JONATHAN EDWARDS

To The Rising Generation

*Addresses Given to Children
and Young Adults*

by

Jonathan Edwards

Compiled and Edited by
Dr. Don Kistler

Soli Deo Gloria Publications
. . . for instruction in righteousness . . .

Soli Deo Gloria Publications
A division of Ligonier Ministries, Inc.
P.O. Box 547500, Orlando, FL 32854
407-333-4244/FAX 333-4233
www.ligonier.org

*

*

Special acknowledgement is given to Kenneth Minkema and The Works of Jonathan Edwards project at Yale University for transcriptions of the manuscripts from which these sermons were retypeset and edited.

*

ISBN 1-57358-168-2

*

Library of Congress Cataloging-in-Publication Data

Edwards, Jonathan, 1703-1758.
  To the rising generation : addresses given to children and young adults / by Jonathan Edwards ; compiled and edited by Don Kistler.
    p. cm.
  ISBN 1-57358-168-2 (alk. paper)
  1. Children–Religious life–Sermons. 2. Youth–Religious life–Sermons. 3. Congregational churches–Sermons. 4. Sermons, American. I. Kistler, Don. II. Title.
  BV4315.E34 2005
  252'.53–dc22

                                      2005004648

Contents

Preface

Jonathan Edwards preached a sermon in the late 1730s to the young people in his congregation, to his young flock, the doctrine of which was "It behooves young persons to seek that they may be converted while they are young." For years before the Great Awakening, Edwards had been telling the children (those under the age of 14) and the youth (those between 14 and 25 years of age) to seek salvation. And he had promoted the idea of early piety through early conversions.

The pastor of the Northampton church preached 30 sermons during his tenure there to children and youth. The difference between Edwards' "childrens' sermons" and today's "childrens' sermons" is striking. One notable reason was the strong possibility that the children and youth of Edwards' day would not have a long life; so he talked with them at length about death and hell. As James Janeway said in his classic evangelistic work, *A Token for Children,* "Parents, your children are not too young to die, and they are not too young to go to hell." Edwards believed this and preached it. For children it was not "justification by death alone."

Here are some of Jonathan Edwards' sermons for children and young people. Four of them have been recently published, three in the Yale University Press volumes of previously unpublished sermons. Nine of the sermons here presented have never been published before. Edwards' "Letter to a Young Convert" is worth adding to any collection of material for the young.

May God use this work to convict little sinners and help turn them into little saints.

Dr. Don Kistler

1

Early Piety Is Especially Acceptable to God

(Preached at a private meeting in November 1734)

"And he did that which was right in the sight of the Lord, and walked in the ways of David, his father, and declined neither to the right hand nor to the left; for in the eighth year of his reign, while he was yet young, he began to seek after the God of David his father."

2 Chronicles 34:2–3

In the words observe three things:

1. The thing in general that Josiah is commended for: he did that which was right in the sight of the Lord. This implies that he was sincere and upright, and a truly holy person. There is a great deal of difference between doing that which is right in the sight of men and doing that which is right in the sight of the Lord; for "God seeth not as man seeth: man looketh on the outward appearance, but God looketh on the heart" (1 Samuel 16:7).

2. It is particularly explained how he did that which was right in the sight of the Lord: he walked in the ways of David, his father, and declined not to the right hand nor the left. When it says that he declined not, it does not mean that he had no failings; for we have an account of a very notable failing of his in his going up to fight with Pharaoh Necho when he had no call to do so (2 Chronicles 35:20–24), which was the occasion of his death. But the meaning is that he was universal in his obedience; he willfully lived in no sin nor did he

neglect any duty.

3. There is special notice taken of a particular instance wherein he did what was right in the sight of the
Lord: he sought God in his youth. "In the eighth year
of his reign, while he was yet young, he began to seek
after the God of his father." We are told in the first
verse that he was eight years old when he began to
reign. So he was about sixteen years old when he began
to seek after the God of David, his father. We find that
this is taken notice of with special commendation, as
being a thing wherein he especially did what was right
in the sight of the Lord, as aceptable and well-pleasing
in God's sight, that he would devote himself to God
when he was thus in his youth.

**DOCTRINE: Early piety is especially acceptable to
God.**

Any excellent endowments and qualifications seem
to be peculiarly amiable in those who are in their
youth. They are more taken notice of by men in such
than in others. So it is in natural endowments: when a
young person appears forward and of prompt and
promising abilities, this is much taken notice of. So it
is in moral qualifications: if a young person is sober
and remarkable for moral motives, it makes him especially lovely in the sight of men. It seems to have a peculiar loveliness in that age.

Therefore we are told of Christ Himself, that when a
young man came to him who was a moral person, Jesus,
beholding him, loved him (Mark 10:21). It was especially lovely to Him to see an endowment in a young
person.

And when a young person has not only morality, but
true grace, this is especially lovely in the sight of God
Himself. It is most peculiarly pleasing and acceptable
to Him.

REASON 1. Those who are pious early dedicate the

flower of their life to God. The flower of our life is due to God; the whole of it is due to God, but God especially challenges the prime of life. All that we have we should give to God, but He is especially pleased when we give our best to Him.

Our youth is on several accounts the best part of our lives. Then nature is in its bloom, farthest from any decay; then the body is most lively, active, and beautiful, and the powers of the mind are in some respects more sprightly. And it is very pleasing to God when persons offer Him such a sacrifice as themselves in their youth, as it was most acceptable to Him when Abel brought the firstlings of his flock (Genesis 4:4). It is like bringing the first fruits to God. The children of Israel were commanded to bring their first ripe fruits and offer them to God (Exodus 22:29).

There is a peculiar honor done to God when persons devote their youthful age to God. This is more to the glory of God than it is to spend all the best of life in the service of Satan, and in slavery to lust, and then to come in our old age and offer to God an old, decayed body and mind that have been almost worn out in the service of sin, so that there shall be nothing left for God but Satan's leftovers.

The devil is sensible that when persons give their youth to God, this is peculiarly to God's honor; and therefore he ever seeks to rob God of this honor and to assume it to himself. So he strives by all possible means to draw and tempt young people to give their youth to him. The devil seems especially, as it were, to delight and glory to have that age of youth for his own, and hence he is commonly so very busy with young people. Hence histories give us an account that in those heathen nations where the devil is worshipped as god, he requires his worshippers to offer human sacrifices to him; he requires that those who are offered in sacrifice to him should be young persons. They must be in their youth. He will accept no other than those who are in their youth. Even in places where the gospel is preached, it is plain to see that Satan's great strife is to have the young people for his own.

REASON 2. It is what is especially pleasing to God because it is exceedingly most suitable that we should begin our lives with God. All things should begin with God, for He is the beginning of all things. He is the Alpha and the Omega (Revelation 1:11), the First and the Last. He is the Creator of all things. He is the Fountain of all being and of all good. He is the Chief Being, the most excellent and worthy Being.

To begin our lives with God is but a suitable acknowledgment of our origin, of the God who has formed us. When a creature is made, his first respects ought to be to his Maker. When God has made a rational creature, the first exercise of reason ought to be given to God. When God has given a creature a power of will, the first exercise of that power ought to be to choose the Being who gave it. When we are setting out, we ought to set out with God, to fix His service and glory as the scope and aim of our whole lives. And therefore God has so ordered things that He has left the time of youth more free and vacant of other cares and concerns than any other time of life, so that persons might have the better opportunity then to attend to the business of religion, if they will but improve it.

REASON 3. When persons are pious early, more of their life is given to God than if they began later; and upon this account early piety is peculiarly acceptable. They who give their youth to God give more of their lives to Him than if they began later; so doubtless they offer the best sacrifice who offer most of their lives to God. It is better to spend the greater part of the life in God's service than only a little at the latter end.

REASON 4. By this means a great deal of sin is prevented. When people don't give their youth to God, but spend it all in sin and the service of the devil, what a sin do such people commit. How much willful sin, how many dreadful provocations, what great guilt do such contract, what uncleanness, and the like?

But how much of this would be prevented if they sought and feared the Lord early, if they repented of sin and forsook it, and heartily yielded themselves to God and His service? A great deal of rebellion, ingratitude, and high contempt of God would be prevented. And as God hates sin and is of purer eyes than to behold evil (Habakkuk 1:13), and cannot look on iniquity, so early piety must be peculiarly acceptable to Him on this account because it prevents so much sin.

REASON 5. Such are more likely to be imminent in holiness. They have more time to grow in grace, and not only that, but they also have more advantages in that they haven't those hindrances to growing in grace that others have. If persons live long in sin, though they are converted at last, yet they still have the ill habits that they contracted while they lived in sin. Those sins were so riveted onto them that grace doesn't perfectly root them out, and they will be a great disadvantage and hindrance. They will be enemies that grace will always have to struggle with as long as they live. And ten to one they will oftentimes be cast down and thrown over by them. They won't be so likely to be Christians of the right sort as those who are converted in their youth.

Application

USE 1. Hence you may learn that God is doubtless more ready to bestow His grace when it is sought when young than afterwards. If it is especially well-pleasing and acceptable to God that young people should be converted more than others, then doubtless God will be more ready to bestow conversion upon conversion on young people when they seek it than others. God will be more ready to bestow converting grace on those who seek it earnestly while young since He loves His own glory; for the conversion of young people is more to the glory of God than the conversion of others. For when young people are converted and give their youth to God, it is more to God's glory, as you have heard already, than when persons turn to God when old.

God is more ready to bestow His converting grace upon young people than others because that is more of a proper season for turning to God, as has been shown already. It is the most proper season for that work of any, and all things are most likely to be obtained if sought in their proper season. If a man would be in the most likely way to obtain a great crop from his land, he must prepare his land and sow his seed in the proper season. Otherwise, it is ten to one whether he succeeds. So those young people who intend sometime or other to be converted had best note this. If you would find God ready to hear and answer when you seek to be converted, take your time to seek it while you are young.

USE 2. If it is especially acceptable to God for persons to turn to early piety, then we may doubtless from hence infer that it is especially for their comfort, seeing that that which is most pleasing to God, God will surely make to be the most for our comfort and happiness. If God takes special delight in early piety, then He will be especially ready to give tokens of His favor and love to those who are pious early. If to be pious early is the way to have most of God's acceptance, then it is also the way to have most of the manifestation of it. If it is the way to have God especially to delight in us, then it

will be the way to have Him to be especially present
with us. If persons are pious early, this is the way to be
favored and blessed with much comfort, peace, light,
and communion with God. And how richly would this
make up for the loss of the pleasures of sin and the vanities of youth! Doubtless there is nothing that tends so
much to the comfort of life while in youth and in old
age as to be pious early.

USE 3. I would earnestly exhort the young people
here present that they would from hence be moved
soon to seek early piety. Consider how reasonable this
is, and here give me leave a little to expostulate. Can
anything be more reasonable than that you should give
God your youth? If you set reason to work, can you
think anything other than that it is foolish for you to
run such a venture as you will do by putting this off?

If you should spend your youth in the sins and vanities of youth, can you rationally think that you shall
thereby get anything that will make your life more
comfortable by it? Can you rationally think that you will
have more comfort and pleasure by this means than if
you spent your life in duties and exercises of piety, or
even that your youth will be more comfortable and
pleasant by it?

Do but consider the nature of those pleasures that
are to be gotten by a life of sin and vanity. What do you
get from outward pleasures? Walking in the ways of religion and virtue don't hinder your taking pleasure in
outward enjoyments, but only in the excess of them, the
abuse of them. And what is gotten by the abuse of
them? And how much sweeter would outward comforts
be if you might enjoy them without fear of hell, the fear
of death, the fear of wrath? And then how much sweeter
would they be with tokens of the favor of God? And how
much more excellent might those pleasures be when
you have the sweetest pleasures?

2

The Sudden Death of Children

(Preached in February 1749/50)

"And when the child was grown, it fell on a day that he went out to his father to the reapers. And he said unto his father, 'My head, my head.' And he said to a lad, 'Carry him to his mother.' And when he had taken him and brought him to his mother, he sat on her knees till noon and then died." 2 Kings 4:18–20

In these words we have recorded an instance of death, concerning which we may observe these two or three things:

1. The person that died: an only child of his parents.
2. At what age: in his childhood, but not in infancy.
3. The manner of his death: very suddenly.

The subject I would now consider and make improvement of is children's liableness to sudden death. All mankind is liable to death by sin, and not only liable to it but must certainly be the subjects of it. Hebrews 9:27: "It is appointed unto men once to die." Job 30:23: "House appointed for all living." Ecclessiastes 9:5: "The living know that they must die."

Death reigns, and no qualifications and no condition of life exempts men.

No strength or art serves to restrain death. And not only are men liable to death, finally to die through the decays of age, but we see that they are liable to death at all ages. Some live very long in the world; they outlive many others. The firmness of their constitution holds

8

till they have buried one generation after another, as if they had clearly escaped and were not subject to the same laws of mortality as others. But yet at last they die.

Men are liable in middle age, in the midst of activity, to die. But some die in their youth, in childhood, in infancy; some die as soon as they are born, nay, some die before they are born.

But I would more particularly consider the liableness of children to die.

Mankind is not only at every age liable to death, but to sudden death. Innumerable are the ways, innumerable are the diseases, very various in their operation. Some are more slow than others, and some are speedy and sudden. Some are, as it were, in a moment, without the least warning. Job 21:23–26: "One dieth in his full strength, being wholly at ease and secure; his pails are full of milk and the marrow of his bones is moist. Another man dies in the bitterness of his soul, never having eaten with pleasure. They lie down alike in the dust, and worms cover them."

Innumerable also are the accidents. These are very arbitrary, sudden in their effect. Many times these things appear as a little thing. It is so with regard to both those kinds of means of death: diseases and accidents. Some diseases at first may appear very small and trivial: a small sore, an aching finger, or some such thing. Oftentimes a very little thing proves an occasion of what we call "accidental death." Sometimes that comes from a very small wound that appeared at first to be no more than a little breach in the skin; or sometimes only the bite of a small insect no bigger than a flea. Sometimes a pin or a some small fragment, or some very small thing accidentally swallowed, shall be sufficient to throw all nature into terrible, violent agonies and struggles, and violently take away life, notwithstanding the utmost that person can do.

Thus the Scripture speaks of being "crushed before the moth" (Job 4:19), and sometimes by such means very suddenly. We have had such an instance this past week: one was taken away suddenly by only swallowing a little piece of a nutshell.

Mankind is liable to sudden death in two respects:

1. They are liable to death by means that are quick in producing their effect. So it was with the child in the text, so it often is with many in regard to diseases that bring on death. Some great disorder suddenly befalls some most vital and essential part of the human frame, as though some main wheel in a machine or the chief spring of the motion had suddenly broken, which ruins the whole at once. Or it is as though something had fallen in and had suddenly interposed itself between the wheels at once to stop all motions. So it often is that accidents prove fatal. So very frequently they produce their effect very speedily.

2. Mankind is liable to sudden death in another respect, and that is that they are liable to death in a season that could not be foreseen. Sometimes death is as sudden as it is unexpected; it comes at a time unlooked for, as a thief comes in the night when men are asleep, lest coming suddenly he finds you sleeping. Then, in this sense, it is common that men are suddenly taken out of the world. The death of the child in the text seems to be sudden in this respect.

But I would more particularly consider childrens' liableness to death, and to sudden death, as to the first two or three years of childhood, even those of infancy. There seem to be more instances of death in that part of the age of men than any other equal part. There are doubtless many more who die in the first two or three years of man's life than any other equal space of time in the life of man, which is very remarkable on some accounts.

This is the very beginning of life, and this is a very great evidence of the doctrine of religion, that of original sin. And though it is not so that death is not so frequent among children after they are gone past their infancy, yet we see they are still very liable to death even after they come to some understanding and strength of body. But while they are yet in their childhood, such are liable to death, and sudden death, as well as others.

It proves to be no security to them that they are at this age, and are at so great a distance from the decay of nature by age. It is no security that 'tis but lately they have received life. It is no security that nature appears to be very flourishing, that the plant is, as it were, in the blossom; that their strength and nature are increasing, and that the faculties of the mind are opening. It is no security that childhood and youth is vanity, and that children are very often...

(The manuscript ends here)

3

The Time of Youth Is the Best Time to Be Improved for Religious Purposes

"Remember now thy Creator in the days of thy youth, while the evil days come not." Ecclessiastes 12:1

These words follow the two last verses of the foregoing chapter, and are part of the same discourse of the wise man: "Rejoice O young man in thy youth. Let thy heart cheer thee in the days of thy youth." The wise man began his counsel to vain, young people in these verses, and our text which as to the next words that follow, are but a continuation of it. In these two last verses of the last preceding chapter, thus he tells the young man what he should not do: "Don't rejoice, O young man, in thy youth, nor let thine heart cheer thee in the days of thy youth." That is, don't allow yourself to indulge in carnal, sinful pleasures and delights. Don't give way to your lusts, to youthful lusts, and gratify them. Don't walk in the ways of your heart and in the sight of your eyes, for know "that for all these things God will bring thee into judgment. Therefore remove sorrow from thine heart and put away evil from thy flesh, for childhood and youth are vanity." That is, "as you would remove sorrow from your heart and evil from your flesh, as you would avoid torment and misery of both body and soul, both here and forever, don't do these things."

And then in the next verse of the text, the wise man tells the young man what he should do: "Remember now thy Creator in the days of thy youth." In these words two things are to be observed:

1. The advice that he gives the young man, which is to remember now his Creator. This advice consists of two parts: (1) that young persons should do this in the day of their youth; (2) and they should do it now, without delay, not putting it off and procrastinating. By this expression we are to understand seeking and serving God, applying himself to the business of religion, and entering into the way of holiness. The probable reason why the wise man expresses it in such terms ("Remember thy Creator") is because those who are in their youth are but lately created; they are newly come out of the hands of their Creator, which is as much as to say, "You who are young and have lately had your being given to you, remember and consider who it is who has given you your being. You who have lately come into the world, remember who brought you into the world. It would be very ill indeed in you who are but newly made if you should forget who made you; if you, as soon as you come out of His creating hands, should turn your backs upon Him and pay no regards to Him who has been forming you."

This was what Israel was blamed for in Deuteronomy 32:15: "He forsook God that made him." Verse 18: ". . . of the Rock that begot thee, thou hast been unmindful." From "remember now thy Creator" it had come to "thou hast forgotten God that begot thee."

2. We may observe the argument with which he began this counsel, implied in these words: "while the evil days come not." There is a twofold reason to enforce the counsel given, implied in these words why young persons should remember their Creator in the days of their youth: because when after your youth,

there will be evil days come upon you. When youth is past, there will come evil days.

Youth is the best and prime morning; it is the prime of our life, and we ought not to turn God off with evil days, days wherein we ourselves have no pleasure. How unreasonable shall we be in expecting that God should have pleasure in them! However, it seems to be signified that the days aren't only evil in themselves, but they are evil for this purpose of remembering to set about engaging in religion. The time of youth is the best time; the days of old age are evil days for any such design. Old age is a very disadvantageous time to seek God, to set about seeking God and salvation in comparison of youth.

The other reason implied here that young persons should act now without delay, that they may do it before the evil days come, intimating that the time of youth is transient and will soon be gone, and the evil days will come. If they put off seeking salvation, these evil days will come upon them before they are aware.

DOCTRINE: The time of youth is the best time to be improved for religious purposes.

The age of man is frequently distinguished into childhood, youth, middle age, and old age. And so youth is distinguished from childhood. But sometimes by youth we understand all that part of the age of man wherein he is young, the whole morning of life, and so it includes both childhood and also the time when persons are young men or women. So it is to be understood in the text, and so would be understood in the doctrine wherein I say that the time of youth is the best time to be improved for religious purposes, and the younger the better after persons have come to the exercise of reason. It is youth that gives the advantages, and the greater that youth is, still the greater the advantage. The time when persons are children, young men and women, is an excellent time; and the time when they are children is yet a time of greater advantage after they are more capable of understanding the principles and rules of religion. Yea, the days of youth in the text mean the whole time of being young, so as to include childhood and youth, as is evident by the foregoing verses.

The time of youth is the best time in these following respects:

1. Such persons ordinarily have the freest opportunity to spend their time in seeking God and their salvation. An infinitely wise God seems to have ordered it so on purpose. We are all born in sin; we come into the world estranged from God, but there is an opportunity through Christ for our recovery. And God has so ordered it that we should have a free and convenient opportunity in the beginning of our lives so that we here may soon get out of that miserable condition in which we are born.

2. It is fitting that we should begin our lives with God; and the first business persons should enter upon should be getting into a converted state and condition. Therefore God has so ordered it in providence that in the beginning or morning of our lives there should be room left for it. There is a vacant space left in the beginning, a time of leisure not filled up with the other cares and business, to give the better and freer opportunity for this business; for God expects that we should do this business first. Persons have ordinarily abundantly freer opportunity, freer from those cares and hurries that come upon persons afterwards. Providence has filled up all the rest of our lives with cares, but here it has left, as it were, a vacant space on purpose that we might begin in the first place with that great business.

Now when this shows that it is the best time, time especially laid out by God for this work, both in word and providence for this work, we must conclude that it should be in every way the best time. And what a pity it is to lose this time, to let it slip. Now when persons have a great deal more time, and a freer opportunity to devote themselves to reading, prayer, meditation, and seeking God; when they are under far greater advantages to do it without distraction—if persons let their youth slip away, ordinarily they'll never find another such time of leisure, and so free an opportunity again.

Sometimes young people think they shall have a better opportunity after their youth is past; they think that they shall have so many things to take their minds off then. But how rarely is it that any find it so; how few what will own that they had the contrary.

3. It is a time wherein persons most easily receive impressions of the great things of religion. Stupidity and hardness of heart increase upon persons as they grow older in sin. It is ordinarily a much more easy thing to affect the mind of a sinner in youth than one who is old in sin. If such persons engage in their great work in their youth, they will be a great deal more likely to get good by awakening sermons and awakening providences, and to have thorough convictions. It is a thing of vast consequence to persons who are seeking salvation that they should have thorough convictions. Many seek a long time, and without these they won't strive and be in good earnest in their great work. Many seek a long time and never are persuaded for want of thorough convictions. Most of those spoken of in Luke 13:24 who shall seek to enter in shall not be able to.

Ordinarily, those persons who seek salvation in their youth haven't done so much to harden and stupify their hearts as others will have done; they haven't sinned so often against their consciences. The more often acts of sin are repeated against conscience, the more softness there is to sin in the conscience. Those who sin against conscience haven't stood it out and bore so many against so many warnings and awakening sermons, and stood against so many awakening providences which, if persons stand out against them, exceedingly tends to stupify the heart. Nothing hardens the heart so much as that which is most awakening. Ordinarily, those who seek salvation haven't stifled so many convictions. The more convictions have been stifled, the less likely persons are to have them.

Persons who seek salvation haven't been guilty of so much backsliding. When persons have begun in a way of religion, and then have backslidden, they are always left worse than before. And their hearts are abundantly harder and more stupid then, and they are less likely to have impressions made on their minds than they were before. That is what the Scriptures teach us again and again, that the last state of man is worse than the first (Matthew 12:45; 2 Peter 2:20).

4. The time of youth is the likeliest time to have God's assistance and blessing in the great business of religion, seeking salvation. As we have observed already, this is a time that God has more especially laid out and designed for that business; and therefore it is most likely that God will afford His assistance and blessing in that time that He has especially laid out for the work. And persons who are still in their youth haven't committed so much sin, and haven't provoked God to that degree they will have done if they put off seeking salvation. Though God's mercy is sovereign and suffices for the pardon of all sin, yet the more the person's guilt is, the more the danger is that God will be provoked to leave persons to themselves.

God gives special encouragement in His Word to those who seek Him early (Proverbs 8:34). And "Those that seek Me early shall find Me" (Proverbs 8:17). This is found by experience, that God seems to be more ready to afford His assistance, and to give success to

early seekers; for the much greater part of those who
are ever converted are those who seek in their youth.
They are especially called and invited by Christ. It is a
much more rare thing to see an old seeker succeed
than one who is in his youth. Others are called, but the
young especially. How often we find wisdom directing
herself to young persons.

Again, reformation is a great deal easier in youth. It
is a great deal easier for persons to thoroughly break
off their sins and to thoroughly reform when in youth
than afterwards. Whenever persons would seek salvation with success, they must thoroughly break off all
their sins and deny their lusts. It is here that many
stick, and it is here that multitudes perish. They can
never be brought to a thorough reformation; this is a
block in their way that they never get over. They are so
wedded to their lusts that they can never consent to
thoroughly part with them. Once persons are brought
to a real, thorough reformation, they are brought a very
great step towards salvation; but, indeed, not many are
brought to this place, and especially not many if the
work isn't done, if thorough reformation isn't done
while they are young.

It is very difficult to thoroughly reform lust at any
time. Men's lusts are naturally so violent and so en-
rooted. But 'tis the older persons' lusts that are the
more difficult. The longer lusts are gratified, continued, and allowed, the more stubborn they grow. The
habits of sin are exceedingly strengthened by long custom, and they grow more and more mature, like a
plant. It is easier plucking up the tree by the roots while
it is still a little bush than after it has stood a long time
and has sent forth its roots deep into the earth. Persons
are more loath and backward to reform, they are less
inclined to go against the grain, they are more indisposed to go about such work as violently, if they are

older. If they are indisposed now, and are unwilling
now to break off their sins, how much more indisposed
will they be when they are older to go about a diligent
observance of all duties of religion? Jeremiah 13:23:
"Can the leopard change his spots, or the Ethiopian
his skin color?"

Oftentimes young persons are ready to think they
shall have a better time after their youth is past, that it
will be easier to reform then. But they only delude
themselves. They may be more out of the way of some
particular temptations, or not so liable to the violent
raging to gratify a particular lust, but as for sin in general, they will doubtless commit it, and its evil habits
will be abundantly strengthened and confirmed.

5. Early piety is especially acceptable unto God. It
must be when persons dedicate to Him the flower of
their age, their prime strength, their vigor, their first
fruits. They who dedicate themselves entirely to God
early give their whole lives to God, which must be more
acceptable to Him than to dedicate only a small part at
the latter end after they have given the greatest part of
their lives to sin and Satan.

They who give their lives to God early are likely to
have more opportunity to serve and glorify God. It is
much more to the honor of God when persons seek
Him in the first place, serving God with their first
fruits. Abel very much honored God, and his sacrifice
was acceptable when he brought the firstlings of his
flock.

It is a most becoming, pleasant sight to see one in
his youth so loving and serving God, and walking as a
child of God. So it is too a pleasant sight to Jesus Christ,
when it is so very pleasing and acceptable to God.

6. Those who are converted when young have great
advantages above others for peace and happiness, for
comfort in this life and happiness forever. They lay a

foundation for solid peace and comfort all their lives, and for time afterwards. When others will have the bitter reflecting on a youth spent in sin, these will have the comfort of reflecting that they, by God's grace, have given their youth to God.

As early piety is especially pleasing and acceptable to God, so there is a probability of His rewarding it with more of the light of His countenance, with testimonies of His favor, with sweet communion with Himself. These will have greater opportunities to grow in grace, and so to obtain assurance, and to lay a good foundation for peace and comfort when they come to die.

They are likely to have opportunity to do more for the honor and glory of God while they live, more time to serve Him, and to do more good works. And so they will have an opportunity to obtain a higher degree of glory; for everyone shall reap according to what he sows (2 Corinthians 9:6).

Application

The use is of exhortation to the young people here present to improve the time of their youth for religious purposes. Make religion the business of your youth. Improve this opportunity for seeking your God and your salvation. You are all children of wrath, since you came into the world, not at peace with God. The great God is angry with you; you are exposed to eternal destruction in hell with the devil and his angels. Be beseeched to improve this opportunity in good earnest to be engaged in that great work of seeking your salvation.

Now you have a great advantage for it above others in that you are yet young. We should prize and make much of the least advantage in an affair that is of such infinite necessity and weight. The least advantage for obtaining eternal salvation, how much it is worth none can tell; for obtaining salvation is a difficult thing, attended with great difficulties—and but few ever obtain it. We may therefore well be glad of anything that in the least puts us under greater advantages to obtain it. Men value a small advantage to get an addition to their estate or money. But how much more valuable is an advantage to get salvation? And yours is not only a small advantage, but a very great advantage above others. You have vastly greater advantages in your hands to get saved from hell and to get to heaven than those who are old. What madness will it be to throw away such an advantage when God gives it to you and puts it into your hands!

There are a number of you here present, and you all, every one of you, have precious and immortal souls, souls that, though it is not long since they were made, yet once are made will last forever and ever in some condition. There is no return for your precious souls into their first nothing; if you should never so much desire it and long for it, it would be impossible. Though you are young, yet the remaining part of your life is but a little while; 'tis but a little while before you will all be in eternity. It may seem a great while to you now, but when eternity comes it will seem a mere nothing, a vanity. Within fifty years, in all probability, most of your souls will be in eternity. They will be disposed of; they will be in those places where they will continue to be forever and ever. It is not to be supposed that they will all be in heaven; yea, it would be a rare thing if half of them should be in heaven.

Everyone of you is ready to flatter himself that your soul shall not be one of those that shall be in hell. If you are in an a natural state, you don't know where you shall be, but the time is hastening when you will know where you must dwell forever, whether in the lake that burns with fire and brimstone or at God's right hand where are pleasures forevermore. If you should end up in the lake where there are everlasting burnings, then you will be sensible of what a precious opportunity your youth was.

Consider that we may rationally conclude that there are some of you here present who will never have any other opportunity but your youth; this is not only the most advantageous and best opportunity that ever you will have, but it is without doubt the only opportunity that some of you will have. 'Tis not to be supposed that all of you will live past your youth; you don't know who of you they are who are never to see any other time but the time of youth in this life. Those who think least of it should be warned, but all of you need to prepare.

Consider how provoking it is to God for persons to spend their youth in sin, for persons to rob Him of the first fruits of the flower, of the prime of that life and the prime morning which God has given them, to spend that time in sin which He has especially appointed for religion.

God especially commands and requires young men to remember their Creator. God often directs Himself to such in Proverbs in such expressions as, "My son, give Me thine heart. My son, observe My ways and lay up My commandments with thee," and many other like passages. He has particularly threatened that He will bring young people into judgment, and told them that to spend their youth in sin is the way to procure sorrow to the heart and evil to the flesh, as in the two last verses of the preceding chapter.

Experience teaches that when persons spend their youth in sin, God often leaves them to hardness of heart all their lifetime after. God is provoked by how many sin away their youth and flatter themselves that they will seek God when their youth is past. But God is provoked by their presumption and leaves them to go on as they have been. But "their bones are full of their youthful vigor" (Job 20:11), and will never stir them up to forsake the sins of their youth.

Therefore, as you have a desire and hope to escape damnation, be advised to improve your youth; be advised not to put it off at all. Consider the command in the text is, "Remember *now* Thy Creator." If you put it off, even intending to do so only for a little while, ten to one you will put it off till youth is past; and then ten to one you will put it off till life is past.

Consider, what pleasure do you get by sin, and youthful vanity or company?

I will conclude with two directions:

DIRECTION 1. Be advised to carefully avoid whatsoever has a tendency to either prevent or take the mind off from a deep concern about eternity and the affairs of your soul. There are many things that have this tendency; the world is full of diversions, things that tend to divert and take the mind off from the great concern. Especially there are innumerable temptations of this kind that young people are exposed to. If the world is so full of one thing or another that tends to fill the minds and draw the hearts of young persons, so that oftentimes religious concerns and serious meditations can find no room; and if something of an impression is by any means made, some concerns of mind about the great things of another world is awakened—yet how apt are those diversions to take them off again!

Now be advised, if you ponder the interest of your soul, to avoid such things as have this tendency, as much as in you lies. Particularly be advised much against two things:

1. Be advised against going often into company. I leave it to everyone to consider whether this does not

have a tendency to divert persons from their great concern. I appeal to the experience of everyone who has tried it, whether or not it has not been the case. Has it not been the case that you have been somewhat moved and affected by something that you have heard in the preaching; and as soon as it is over you go into company, which diverts your minds and takes away the impressions that were left there? And if it has the tendency to take off impressions when made, for the same reason it will tend to prevent their being made at all, and will harden the heart against impressions.

2. Be advised against keeping company, against being much conversant with persons who live a vain life, or seem to be wholly regardless of the things of religion. Do not be a companion with such; do not seek their company, but endeavor to avoid being intimate with them. Such tend to make you like themselves. Proverbs 13:20: "He that walketh with wise men will be wise, but the companion of fools will be destroyed."

DIRECTION 2. Use all those methods that have a tendency to fix your thoughts on such concerns, and that lead you to be much thinking of them. I will here mention some:

1. Diligently attend to the preaching of the Word. The Word of God is the great means that God has appointed for our instruction, warning, and awakening, and you can't expect benefit from it by a careless hearing of it. Rather, there will be a danger of its proving to be mischievous. If you would try this method, to be constantly, diligently attentive, 'tis to be hoped it would have an effect to awaken you.

2. Be constant in the duty of secret prayer; 'tis not only an absolute duty, as expressly commanded as any in the Bible, but has a great tendency to keep you from sin.

3. Be much in conversing with the godly, and with

others who are deeply concerned about their salvation. What we talk about we are apt to think on when alone. Seeing others concerned is apt to impress that concern upon us, which we shall see by talking with them has a tendency to make us so to. And talking will tend to convince us of the reality of such a thing as condition they are in, and to make us earnestly desire to be in their state.

4. Another thing I would advise is private religious meetings. If young people, instead of meeting to gather to drink or to frolic, would meet from time to time to read and to pray to God, and together to seek their salvation, doubtless it would have a great tendency to more and more lead them to think of it and to fix their minds on it. This would be found a great help to them, and this is the best way they can help one another.

4

The Sins of Youth Go with Them to Eternity

(To the young people at a private meeting, March 1733)

"His bones are full of the sins of his youth, which shall lie down with him in the dust." Job 20:11

Zophar is here in this chapter setting forth the misery and doleful state of a wicked man, and that, however he may seem for a while to prosper in the world, his triumphing is short (Job 20:5-8), and his joy is but for a moment. And though his excellency mounts up to the heavens and his head reaches unto the clouds, yet he shall perish forever like his own dung, and he shall fly away as a dream and shall not be found. He shall be chased away as a vision of the night and he shall not only be followed with the wrath of God, but judgment shall pursue his posterity. "His children shall seek to please the poor, and his hands shall restore their goods" (Job 20:10).

In the text the misery of the wicked man is spoken of in this life, and after his death 'tis spoken of by reason of his sins yet attending Him still and following him to his grave. 'Tis a doleful thing for persons to die in their sins, to have all the load of their sins, the sins that they have been guilty of, attending of them, lying upon their souls at such a time as when they are dying, and to carry them out of the world with them.

In these words we may observe:

1. What sins of the wicked man we have spoken of,

the sins of his youth.

2. How they attend the wicked man: they attend him, and he carries them out of the world with him. The sins of his youth are with him and upon him when he comes to die; he carries them with him to his grave and when he goes into eternity. This is expressed in the text in two ways:

First, that his bones are full of these sins. By "his bones" is meant his dead body, his corpse.

Second, that they lie down with him in the dust. This is as much as to say that when he lays his bones in the grave, they are full of the sins of his youth.

That this is the meaning of it is confirmed by a parallel text in Ezekiel 32:27: "And they shall not lie with the mighty that are fallen of the uncircumcised which are gone down to hell with their weapons of war, and they have laid their swords under their heads, but their iniquity shall be upon their bones, though they were the terror of the mighty in the land of the living." It is evident that by their iniquity being upon their bones is meant that they shall remain on their bodies; not that their sins will properly be lying down with them in the dust or will remain upon the dead corpse. Sins can't be upon a dead corpse because the dead body is not capable of sin. The sins that is upon the soul goes into the eternal world. This is only a figurative expression to signify that wicked men's sins don't leave them when they die, but remain with them after they are dead. They abide with them as long as they live; and not only so, but they remain with them after they are dead; they lie down with them in the grave.

Both these expressions in the text signify the same thing, that his bones are full of the sins of his youth, and that they shall lie down with him in the dust, that is, he shall carry the sins of his youth to the grave with him; and when his bones are laid in the grave, then his sins shall lie down with him and remain in his bones.

It is said that his bones are full of the sins of his youth rather than his dead body is full of them to more emphatically signify how wicked men's sins will everlastingly abide with them after death, the bones being what remain longest of any part of the dead corpse. This is as much as to say that death can't free men from sin, but their sin is still upon them when they are dead; sin lies down with them in the dust and there remains upon them; and when the flesh has rotted off their bones and is turned to dust, their sin still remains upon them, their iniquity is still upon their bones.

Such figurative representations of eternal things are more frequently made use of in the Old Testament because a future and eternal state was not then so fully revealed as it is now. The sins of youth seem there to be particularly mentioned because persons oftentimes spend that age very much in sin, and the more emphatically to show and to signify how wicked men's sins are and how abiding the guilt of sin is. The sins that were committed in youth, in the beginning of life, the guilt of them does not wear out. If they live till they are old, it remains; it follows them to the grave and remains upon their bones after they are dead.

Their bones are said to be full of sin to signify how much sin wicked men are guilty of. The heart of a wicked man is full of sin, brimfull. This is to express how much sin many persons are guilty of in their youth. Their youth abounds with iniquity, and their guilt upon that account abounds, and their punishment abounds after they are dead.

DOCTRINE: Many persons never get rid of the guilt of the sins of their youth, but it attends them to their graves and goes with them to eternity.

PROPOSITION 1. Many persons spend the time of their youth in sin. Though the time of youth is the best

time that men ever have to seek their salvation in and
to secure the everlasting good of their souls, yet it is
common for men to spend this season of life in sin and
vanity. The spiritual and eternal concerns are very often
neglected by young people. They don't trouble their
heads much about death and another world. They
choose to spend their youth in pursuit of ease and in
pleasure. They put off the great concern of their souls.
They seem, many of them, to think that religion better
fits older persons than them. They look upon religion
as a dull, melancholy sort of thing. They can see no
pleasure that is to be had in it. It seems to them to have
a tendency only to make their lives uncomfortable; and
though they may design sometime or other to mind the
concern of their souls and to seek their salvation, yet
they think this work is more suitable for men when
they begin to grow old, if they think anything about it
at all.

Indeed, some young persons seem to be so inconsiderate and careless that they scarcely think or care
anything about it. They seem as if they never had any
serious thoughts about their salvation, and the necessity of turning to God in order to obtain it. And so it
may be that they scarcely have any design of seeking
salvation either now or hereafter. They don't go as far
in their thoughts as to come to any determinations.

Their minds are upon other things; they are taken
up with vanity. And when they go to meetings and hear
sermons, they take so little notice of what they hear, or
think so little about it, that the most awakening discourses are scarcely enough to raise the least concern
in them about their own condition, or to put them
upon any thoughts about it. It may be all the while that
there they hear the sound in the meetinghouse when
the minister is preaching, yet they are thinking of
something else and don't mind what is said. And if

they sometimes happen to turn a thought upon the concern of their souls, yet they flatter themselves that they are now young and there will be time enough hereafter. Death looks a great way off to them because they are young, and they let future time take care of itself for the present. They hope some way or the other they shall find means to escape and get converted before they die. For the present they will choose to mind other things.

Youth is a time of temptation. Man has a corrupt nature as soon as he has a being, and yet men don't come into the world at all fortified against temptation, but with principles that are ready to betray them to all manner of temptation—and youth is a time of great temptation. The world and its vanities look gay and tempting in the eyes of young people; they are ready to entertain a great opinion of the vain delights of the world, and these things are ready to take up all their thoughts.

Often young people are commonly one another's enemies. They tempt and they harden one another and draw one another to sin. Ill company proves a great snare to many young people when they first come abroad in the world, and a snare that many of their souls are taken in and never escape. It is a snare that the devil takes them in and carries them to hell.

Satan the more easily prevails with young people by reason of their inconsiderateness and want of experience. They often do things in their youth that causes exceeding bitterness to them all their lifetime after when more experience shows the mischief of it.

And thus many young people spend their youth in sin. Ecclesiastes 11:10: "Childhood and youth are vanity." And some, while in their youth, fall into gross sins, yea, live in grossly wicked practices. Some while in their youth spend their time in profaneness; some spend their youth in impurity and practice uncleanness; they live in a continual indulgence of unclean imaginations, exercising their lusts and fomenting their thoughts. And not only so, but they are impure in their language and conversations with their companions, who are also grossly impure in their sinful practices.

PROPOSITION 2. Many persons never get rid of or are freed from the guilt of the sins that they thus commit, but they carry it with them to their graves and into eternity. From their youth till they are very old, the guilt of these sins abides with them. There it is upon them when they lie gasping and dying, and their souls go into eternity to appear before God full of the guilt of those sins. The reasons are these:

Reason 1. God doesn't excuse them because they were in their youth. Many seem to be bold in wickedness when in their youth because they think it is excusable by reason of their age; they seem to think youth a proper time to be wicked in; they are now in their youth, and therefore think themselves more excusable. They think it is not to be expected that they should be otherwise. They say that it is not to be expected that they should be so sober and serious as elderly people. They say, "We must not expect grey hairs on green shoulders." And many in this vicious and corrupt world are so ready in too great a degree to flatter and excuse young people in their sins. They will make light of their extravagances and say, "They are young, inconsiderate, and foolish now, but may make very good men for all that."

But it is not this vicious and corrupt world, it is not men, but God who is to be their Judge; and He won't excuse them for their wickedness because they were in their youth. Such a plea as this avails nothing before God. Men may quiet their consciences with it now, but they can't satisfy their Judge with it. God marks the sins of their youth. He observes how negligent they are of their souls, and how they give way to their lusts. He seals up their trangression as in a bag. He remembers them and will call them to an account for all their sins of youth. Ecclesiastes 11:9: "Rejoice, O young man, in thy youth, and let thine heart cheer thee in the days of thy youth; walk in the ways of thine heart and in the sight of thine eyes. But know that for all these God will bring thee into judgment."

Reason 2. God doesn't forget their sins of youth, though they were committed so early and though they live a long time after. If men should live to grow old, if they should spend 50 or 60 years afterwards before they die, yet none of their sins of youth are forgotten. The account of them that is written in God's book of remembrance (Malachi 3:16) doesn't fade. Men themselves are ready in a great measure to forget the sins of their youth when they come to grow in years. If the acts themselves are not gone out of their memory, yet they cease to trouble their consciences as once they did. They don't think much about their sins of youth; it was a great while ago, and things are very altered since then, and so they seem to think that they have no more to do with the sins that they committed then. But it is not so with God. He remembers all and will require all the guilt of every idle word (Matthew 12:36), and every light, vain, or impure act. It remains as full and requires as heavy a punishment as it did the first hours or minutes after they committed it.

Reason 3. It very often comes to pass that they, having spent their youth in sin, and so missed their best time for conversion, are never converted afterwards. The time of youth, as we are often taught, is the best time for seeking the grace of God. It has peculiar encouragements given to us in the Word of God (see Ecclesiastes 11:9 and 12:1; Mark 10:15; Luke 18:17).

When persons spend their youth in sin, neglecting their souls, then it very often comes to pass that they never are converted afterwards. Such an opportunity for conversion as the time of youth is, once it is passed, never comes again. If persons would improve the time of youth as they might do, they might ordinarily obtain conversion; but if they let that slip and sin it away, their best time gets by, and so very often they never do obtain salvation at all, and so bring the sins that they committed in their youth to the grave with them. "They lie down in the dust with them, and their bones are full of them."

Reason 4. Oftentimes persons, by the sins of their youth, quench the striving motions of the Spirt they have then and so never have them again. Persons in their youth are ordinarily more easily awakened than afterwards; their minds are more tender, and it is an easier thing to make impressions upon them.

It is a more common thing for natural men to have the motions and strivings of the Spirit when they are young than afterwards. God begins to work upon their minds while they are but beginning their lives. And persons, by their sins of their youth, oftentimes quench those strivings of the Spirit of God. God sometimes comes by His Spirit, striving with persons while in their youth; more than once He is repelled and His motions are quenched. But before their youth is passed, He comes again and does, as it were, give them another offer. But if they quench and stifle the convictions of the Spirit of God by giving way to youthful temptations and pursuing youthful vanities, and so sin away their youth, sometimes the Spirit of God never returns anymore to them. Being repelled, and because of their ungodly practices, He leaves them finally, and so their sins forever cleave to them; they are never converted; they never have any true repentance given them of their sins of youth, and so they lie down with them in the dust.

Reason 5. God is often prvoked by their sins of youth, either to cut them off in their youth or to give them up to sin. It is very provoking to God when persons spend their youth in sin. God particularly requires and insists upon it that persons should give their youth, the prime of their life to Him (Ecclesiastes 12:1). God requires this as He required the first fruits of old (Exodus 23:19). And however light many persons may make of the sins of youth, God is dreadfully provoked when young people follow their lusts regardless of Him.

We have various instances in Scripture of God's wrath for the sins of young people. How remarkably He showed His wrath towards Onan (Genesis 38:8-10), and against Phinehas and Hophni for their wickedness while young (1 Samuel 2:34). How He showed His wrath against the children who reviled Elisha (2 Kings 2:23–24), though they were but children. And there are many who are, for the sins of their youth, cut off and sent to hell while in their youth. Others are given up to hardness of heart who have been wicked in their youth. Many such have lived till they have grown old and have never shown any considerable signs of awakening till their dying day; and if they live, they are but reserved for a heavier condemnation (Genesis 15:16; Revelation 14:7).

Reason 6. Persons, by spending their youth in sin, get such a custom of sinning and strengthen the habits of sin that it lays them under a great disadvantage regarding the good of their souls ever after. The time of youth is a person's forming time. Impressions that are made in youth are the deepest and most lasting; the way that persons get accustomed to while young they are most difficultly brought out of. It is most hard to forsake a custom that is gotten in youth and that has, as it were, grown up with a person.

Many times persons, by giving way to sin when young, get those customs of sinning that they never leave as long as they live. "Can the Ethiopian change his skin?" (Jeremiah 13:23). And if they don't continue in that particular custom of sin, yet all the habits of sin are mightily strengthened and confirmed by a sinful course of life in youth. The heart is dreadfully hardened, and Satan's interest is greatly and dreadfully established, so that they never forsake their ways of sin, and therefore bring their sins of youth to the grave and into eternity with them.

Application

USE OF SELF-EXAMINATION. Let these points put those young persons who are present upon examining themselves as to whether or not they are not going on in sinful courses. Are you not spending away your youth, your most precious season of life, in sin? Don't you live negligent of your precious soul in the neglect of secret prayer and other duties required of you? Aren't you now guilty of putting off seeking your salvation till hereafter, being willing to take your ease and pleasure in the time of your youth? Are you not living in a very sinful and provoking neglect of the known duties of religion? Are you not spending your time, and are you not guilty of going on in ways that are unwarrantable? Do you not spend your time in vain company? Do you not associate yourselves with those whom you know are persons of a vain conversation, and who are not only a snare to you to stir you up to sin, in whose company you get no good, but only hurt? Are they not an occasion of a great deal of sin in you? Are you not guilty of using your tongue in a wicked manner, in profane or unclean language when you are with your companions? Don't you live in the allowance of sinful, wicked thoughts and imaginations? Don't you give your lusts and imaginations unbridled liberty in your thoughts?

Persons may be guilty of a great abundance of wickedness in their thoughts, by which they may dreadfully provoke the Most High to anger. Yea, are you not guilty of some practice or another that is unwarrantable, that you would not dare to stand in if you were going to die, or were immediately to appear before the judgment seat of God?

What effect have the many warnings that are given you in the preaching of the Word had upon you? Do you regard them? Are they not slighted by you? Don't you make light of what you often hear of your duty and of your danger? Are you not now going on in such ways as these without any serious design of altering your course of life?

Let me entreat everyone now to examine himself, and if the case is thus with you, then let me entreat you seriously to consider what you have heard at this time. Consider what danger there is that the present sins of your youth, however light you make of them, will lie down with you in the dust, and what danger there is, what reason you have to fear, that you are now contracting that guilt that you will never get rid of, but will carry with you as long as you live. If you should live to be never so old, those sins will be with you when you lie gasping and struggling with the pangs of death. They will go with your poor, miserable soul into eternity when you go to appear before God.

The sins that you are now daily committing, and that you make so light of, aren't such light matters as you are ready to think. They'll be no pleasant things to think when you lie dying. They will not be pleasant when they follow you into another world; they will be

no pleasant companions when you come to stand before God, and the guilt of them will never wear out in
hell. After you have burned in hell a million ages, the
guilt of the sins of your youth will remain as full as ever,
and you will have never the less to suffer for them for
the future for what is suffered already. There will be an
eternity of suffering behind for them and all to as great
a height as ever.

If ever there should come such a time that you
should go out of the world with the sins of your youth,
the first minute of your feeling hell's torments will
make you thoroughly sensible of how vastly mistaken
you were in thinking so lightly of the sins of youth. You
will be sufficiently inclined to believe what ministers
used to tell you about them, however little you believe
them now.

USE OF EXHORTATION. This use is to those who
are in youth not to go on and spend their youth in sin,
but in the practice of virtue and religion. God has made
you reasonable creatures; if you act reasonably and like
reasonable creatures, you will hearken to this advice.
Your reason can't but approve of it and own that as you
regard your own good and happiness, this must be your
best and wisest way, and that it is great folly to do otherwise.

Young persons have many objections against a person forsaking a course of sin and taking themselves to
a life of duty, and above all to a virtous and religious
life. I would therefore here desire you to consider two
things:

1. Consider what a disadvantage it will be to you if
you should spend your youth in sin. Perhaps you
promise yourself ease and pleasure, and you don't care
to deprive yourselves of the way that you are in. You
don't wish to trouble yourself with serious religion.
The ways of youth seem to you to be the most pleasant

way of living.

But you have very mistaken notions of things. If you spend your youth in sin, you will get nothing by it while you live in this world. You are mistaken if you think that you shall make your life more comfortable by it. You can't take a more direct course to lay a foundation for trouble and sorrow while you live in this world than by spending your youth in sin.

If you do but consider the pleasures you get by sin, and the comforts that you think you get by it for the present, they are but poor things. There is so much vexation attending them; there is a great deal of remorse of conscience and many things that sting in them. The sins that you now commit will lay a foundation for an abundance of trouble in the future part of your life. Your sins of youth will prove to be a foundation for bitter reflections all your life. How many persons are there who are now past their youth, and who have cause, with great trouble and bitterness, to think of their misspent youth. What would they not give, if they had now such an opportunity as they had when young, to seek their salvation instead of sin away their youth!

Yea, a youth spent in sinful courses is very often an occasion of persons living all their lifetime uncomfortably with respect to temporal comfort. And what is thus gotten by pursuing pleasure in a way of sin? There are many persons who have a miserable life all their days, and the foundation of it is the sinful courses of their youth; they might otherwise have lived comfortably and honorably, and with abundantly more of the relish of the common blessings of God's providence.

2. If you become pious while young, it will tend to make your youth more abundantly pleasant; it won't spoil the pleasure of your youth, it will increase it. Proverbs 3:17: "Wisdom's ways are ways of pleasantness."

And Proverbs 24:13: "My son, eat thou honey." Though at present you are unexperienced in the pleasures of religion, yet you may rationally conclude that it must be so; for certainly it must be a more pleasant life to have to consider that you are now at peace with God, that God has become your Father and Friend, that you are now safe from hell, that you have an interest in Christ and are ready for death, let it come when it will; that when you die you shall go to heaven to enjoy eternal glory and happiness; that God, while you are here, will take care of you and will give His angels charge concerning you (Matthew 4:6).

And besides all this, at the same time, you are allowed to enjoy the comforts and pleasures of this life, only in God's way and manner, and according to the rules He gives us. Yet you have liberty to taste of the good things of His Providence in such a way as tends most to our delight and comfort.

I say, you may rationally conclude that such a life as this is a much more pleasant life than to go in ways that you know God has forbidden, and to have to think that God is your Enemy, and is angry with you every day. This is more pleasant than to consider that you are in a Christless state, and that if you should die in such a state as you are now in you would go straight to hell; that it must be your portion to burn in hell forever; that you haven't God's blessings with your enjoyments, which are sinful, and to have an accusing conscience flying in your face from time to time.

I speak to you as reasonable creatures, and your reason can't but tell you that this must be a much more uncomfortable and unpleasant life than the other. Your society one with another would be abundantly more pleasant if you always were virtuous in your conversation, and did not keep strictly to rules of virtue in your conversation together. If you tried, you would find and own that it was so.

So you get nothing by spending your youth in sin, but are great losers for the present, besides the danger thay you incur of having your bones full of the sins of your youth when you die, of their lying down with you in the grave, of their following you to God's judgment seat, of their going to hell with you, and then into your eternity.

5

The Most Direct Way to Happiness
(Preached in May 1734)

"My son, eat thou honey because it is good, and the honeycomb which is sweet to thy taste; so shall the knowledge of wisdom be to thy soul when . . ."

Proverbs 24:13–14

We may observe in these words:

1. The manner in which the wise man accosts us: "My son." He often makes use of such a compellation and manner of address in this book; and one reason for it seems to be that he wrote this book more especially for the instruction of young people, as he himself informs us in chapter 1:4: "to give the young man knowledge and discretion." There are some other passages that make it evident that he has the instruction of young people especially in view, particularly the instance given in chapter seven of the young man who was void of understanding, who was deceived by the strange woman. This seems to be a reason why the wise man speaks in such language. In giving these instructions to young people, he takes the part of a father to them, and so addresses them in the language of a father.

Probably the wise man might have a particular aim at the benefit of his own children in these instructions, especially Rehoboam, who was the heir to his crown (1 Kings 11:43).

But there is a further reason to be given why such a

style is used, and that is that the wise man doesn't speak to us in his own name, but it is God who speaks to us by him. Our heavenly Father condescends to instruct and counsel us as a Father. This reason is given by the apostle why such a compellation as "my son" is used in this book of Proverbs when he quotes Proverbs 3:11, as we see in Hebrews 12:5: "And have ye forgotten the exhortation which speak unto you as unto children, 'My son, despise not thou the chastening of the Lord, nor faint when thou art rebuked of Him.'"

2. We may observe the precept or counsel contained in the words, which is to seek and embrace wisdom, or virtue and piety, which is ordinarily intended by wisdom in this book, as the wise man himself tells us in Proverbs 9:10: "The fear of the Lord is the beginning of wisdom, and the knowledge of the holy is understanding."

3. The enforcement of this counsel, that is, because this is the most direct way to the enjoyment of comfort and pleasure. The practice of virtue and piety is sweet enough to be its own reward. The wise man as much as says that it would be well worth our while to live a pious and holy life if it were only for the sake of the pleasure of it. We eat honey because it is good, and the honeycomb because it is sweet to our taste; we eat honey for the pleasure of it. So, says the wise man, it is with respect to piety or wisdom: 'tis as much worth the while to practice this for the sake of the pleasure of it: "so shall the knowledge of the holy be." This is as much as to say, "Whether you believe it or not, yet, if you will make trial, you shall find it to be so; then that shall be a reward; then you shall find that the pleasures of a life of virtue and religion is a good reward by itself." That is, if you make trial of that, you shall not be disappointed; you won't fail of your expectation.

We are still to remember, as has been observed already, that the wise man has a particular respect to young people who especially are wont to seek pleasure.

DOCTRINE: The most direct way that young people can take to spend their youth pleasantly is to walk in the ways of virtue and piety. This may seem very strange, and a great deal paradoxical to many young people, but I hope to make it very evident in the following method:

I would show, first, that spending youth in the practice of religion and virtue is the way to obtain pleasures that are vastly more excellent than are to be found in the way of sin and vanity.

Second, such a course doesn't destroy young people's comfort, or outward enjoyments, but adds to them.

Third, it makes youth the pleasanter in all the circumstances and concerns of it.

1. Hereby young people may obtain vastly more excellent pleasures than by spending their youth in sin and vanity. Hereby they may obtain pleasures that are of a more noble and excellent kind, that are more worthy of the nature of man and more suitable to it, not vile and brutish pleasures, not such as the beasts can partake in with them. But these delights are of a more sublime nature, fit for those who have rational and immortal spirits, and in which they communicate with the heavenly spirits.

Hereby may be obtained pleasures that are more solid and substantial, that aren't like a flash, a blaze, and crackling of thorns, but rather are like the constant shining of the sun. Hereby may be obtained pleasures that are vastly sweeter and more exquisitely delighting, that are of a more satisfying nature, pleasures that are beams, like those in the highest heavens in the soul that exceed the pleasures of the vain and sensual as much as diamonds and gold exceed dirt and dung, and as the light of the sun does the blaze of the meteors of the night.

But here I would mention two or three things to
show that the pleasures that young people may obtain
by following such a course are far better than what are
to be obtained in a life of youthful vanity.

• By embracing religion and virtue young people
may obtain the greatest beauty and the most excellent
ornaments. One way in which young people are wont to
seek pleasure is in adorning themselves, endeavoring
to recommend themselves in a fine appearance. Youth
is a time wherein nature is in its bloom, and young
people are often wont to value themselves by their
beauty and to place their happiness much in outward
ornaments. But by embracing true religion and virtue,
they would have the graces of God's Spirit, the beauty
and ornaments of angels, and the love image of God.
They might obtain that which would render them far
more lovely than the greatest outward beauty possible;
they might obtain that beauty which would render
them lovely in the eyes of all the wise men, the angels
of heaven, the Lord Jesus Christ, and the great God
Himself. They would have those ornaments of the mind
that are more beautiful and glorious than the robes of
princes.

How highly would many young people esteem
themselves if they could well afford to adorn themselves
as some of the great ones of the earth? But even if they
could, these things would be vile in comparison to the
beauty of the graces of God's Spirit, the ornaments of
Christian humility and love, a childlike spirit towards
God, and a spirit of divine love to Christ and to those
who are His. 1 Peter 3:3–4: "Whose adorning let it not
be that outward adorning of plaiting the hair, and of
wearing of gold, or of putting on of apparel; but let it
be the hidden man of the heart, in that which is not
corruptible, even the ornament of a meek and quiet
spirit, which is in the sight of God of great price."

• By walking in the ways of true religion and virtue, young people will obtain the sweetest pleasures, the sweetest delights of love and friendship. A life of true religion and virtue is a life of divine love, a life of love to God, which love affords greater pleasures by far than that of earthly lovers. A life of love is the sweetest life in the world; but no love affords such pleasures as love to God. Divine love is an affection that is of a more sublime and excellent nature than love to an earthly object; it is a purer flame, and the pleasure that it affords is a purer stream.

They who live a life of true piety live a life of love to the Lord Jesus Christ; there is a most dear friendship between Him and them; their souls are espoused to Christ, their hearts are knit to Him, and their love has an infinitely more beautiful and lovely object than that of earthly lovers and their love is not despised, but accepted of Christ. They may freely have acess to Christ at all times to express their love. Song of Solomon 8:1: "O that thou wert as my brother, that sucked the breasts of my mother! when I should find thee without, I would kiss thee; yea, I should not be despised." As those who walk in the ways of religion and virtue love this glorious Person, so they are loved by Him. This divine love is always mutual; there is love on both sides. The love of Christ for them doesn't fall short of theirs to Him, but indeed greatly exceeds it; this love vastly exceeds the love of any earthly lover. Christ has given greater manifestations of love to those who love Him than ever any earthly friend did to the object of his love; for He has died for them and and so has rescued them from eternal destruction and has purchased for them eternal glory.

Those young people therefore who spend their youth in living a life of love to Christ spend their youth the most pleasantly of any young people whatsoever.

1 Peter 1:7–8: "that your faith might be found to praise and glory at the appearing of the Lord Jesus Christ, whom having not seen ye love, in whom though now ye see Him not, yet believing ye rejoice with joy unspeakable and full of glory."

• Young people, by walking in ways of true piety, obtain the sweetest gratification of appetite, not of carnal, sensual appetites, but of those that are more excellent, of spiritual and divine appetites, holy desires and inclinations; those that, as they are more excellent in themselves, are more suitable to the nature of man and are far more extensive, so are capable of gratification and enjoyments more exquisite, sweet, and delightful.

They who truly embrace religion and virtue, there are infused into them new appetites after heavenly enjoyments; and they who walk in a way of holiness obtain in this world the gratification of those spiritual appetites in a degree for the discoveries of God's glory, the views of Christ's beauty, and in the incomes of the Holy Spirit whereby the soul is filled with joy in the Holy Ghost. They feed on angels' food, on the bread which came down from heaven, and have the foretastes of heaven's dainties.

• Those young people who walk in the ways of religion and virtue have the most pleasant company. Young people commonly seek pleasure in company, and oftentimes spend much of their time in mirth among their companions. But none have such delightful company as those who live in the exercise of holiness and virtue, for they have their conversation in heaven (Philippians 3:20). The Lord Jesus Christ has become their Friend and Companion. Oftentimes, when they are alone and seem to the world to spend their time solitarily, they indeed have company enough; it is their delight to withdraw from all the world the more freely and intimately to converse with

Jesus Christ. When someone has a dear friend that he greatly sets his affection upon, he does not much want other company; it will be a pleasure to him to be withdrawn from others and the more fully and freely to enjoy intercourse and conversation with him.

The Father and the Son come to seek young people who walk in God's ways, and will make their abode with them and manifest themselves to them (John 14:21–23). Such young people have an intercourse with heaven; by meditation, prayer, and other duties of religion they, with a spiritual eye, see Christ and have access to Him to communicate their mind to Him. And Christ, by His Spirit, communicates Himself to them so that there is a spiritual conversation between them and Jesus Christ. And must not this needs be the most pleasant and the happiest company? Is not the God who made us able to give us more pleasure in intercourse with Himself than we have in conversations with a worm of the dust?

Thus young people, by walking in ways of religion and virtue, obtain pleasures of the excellent kind.

2. I come now to show that walking in ways of religion and virtue doesn't hinder young people's comfort in outward enjoyments, but promotes it. It gives them a far more excellent kind of pleasure, more sweet and satisfying delights than the world can afford, but the enjoyment of these things doesn't rob young people of pleasure in outward things, but helps it.

Religion doesn't forbid the use of outward enjoyments, but only the abuse of them. It doesn't forbid the enjoyment of outward good things, for they were made to be received with thanksgiving, but only forbids the vicious and irregular manner of enjoying them. There is a way of enjoying outward things that is not disagreeable to the commands of God.

Outward enjoyments are much sweeter, and really afford more pleasure, when regularly used than when abused. Temporal good things are never so sweet, they are never taken with so good a relish, as when they are taken with innocence and in the way of virtue. Vice destroys the sweetness of outward enjoyments. So much as men transgress divine rules by taking outward enjoyments in a forbidden way, and so much as they go beyond the bonds of temperance and moderation in the enjoyment of them, so much is abated from the relish of them. Vice mixes a bitterness in enjoyments and causes a sting to be with the honey. When we enjoy outward good things with innocence, and agreeably to the rules of God's Word, we then enjoy them with peace in our minds; but when they are viciously used, the pleasure is attended with inward remorse. Such a one does not have the approbation of his own conscience in what he enjoys. In order to a person's having any quietness, he must stupify himself and suppress the exercises of reason and keep himself from reflecting; otherwise, he can enjoy his pleasures with no peace.

Besides, when a person who walks in the ways of holiness has the pleasures of outward enjoyments, he has this to give a sweetness and relish, that he has it as the fruit of the love of God.

3. I am come now to the next point, which is to show that the exercise of virtue and religion makes youth the more pleasant in all the circumstances and concerns of it. Herein it greatly has the advantage over a course of youthful vanity, for the pleasures of that are exceedingly unsteady and inconstant; they serve them only for a moment.

Here particularly, young people's exercise of religion would sweeten both their company and their solitude. It would sweeten their company in that it would render it more pleasant. There is nothing gotten by extravagance and lewdness in company. Company is not the more pleasant for it; vain and vicious mirth does company no good; it neither adorns it nor enlivens it. How needless and to what purpose it is. Ecclesiastes 2:2: "I said of laughter, it is mad, and of mirth, what doeth it?" Young people do the devil all that service gratis; they get nothing by it for the present; they undo themselves without so much as getting any pleasure by it presently.

It would be abundantly sweeter if they were virtuous in company; it would be more rational, more becoming reasonable creatures. Their own reason would approve of it; they would be glad when they reflected and thought on it. Everyone's mind would approve of it.

It is a strange notion that many young people have that company will be the worse for being virtuous. Vice is the most useless thing in the world. In company it does no good in any way. They may may have free conversation without it; they may please and entertain themselves better without it, and virtue would sweeten all that is said and done. It would make all the more pleasant company one to another; it would supply them with the most pleasant and entertaining subjects of conversation.

The exercise of this would also sweeten solitude and retirement. Oftentimes those who live viciously and appear very merry in company are afraid of solitude; they don't love to be much in retirement for they have nothing to entertain them. And when they are alone, reason and conscience are apt to be in exercise, which greatly disturbs their peace. But those young people who walk in ways of religion and virtue have wherein to rejoice and to entertain their minds both alone and in company. 'Tis pleasant to them oftentimes to be alone, for then they have the better opportunity to fix their minds on divine objects, to withdraw their thoughts from worldly things, and the more uninterruptedly to delight themselves in divine contemplations and holy exercise and converse with God.

Christ sometimes calls forth such young persons from the company and noise of the world in such language as that found in Song of Solomon 7:11–12: "Come, my beloved . . . ."

It sweetens both business and diversion. To walk in the ways of piety and Christianity is the way to have the sensible presence of God, the light of His countenance, and the testimony of His favor, which is enough to sweeten everything to them. If a person has good evidence that his sins are forgiven, that he is at peace with God, is the object of God's love, and has within him the testimony of a good conscience, this is enough to give quietness and cheerfulness wherever he is and whatever he is about. 'Tis enough to make hard labor easy, and he may well do whatsoever he does cheerfully who does it to the Lord and not to man (Ephesians 6:7).

The exercise of religion would even sweeten young people's diversions as it would regulate them according to the rules of wisdom and virtue, and would direct them to suitable and worthy ends and make them subservient to excellent purposes. What has already been said of earthly enjoyments and company is true of diversions, that they are abundantly sweetest when virtue moderates and guides them.

It sweetens what is present, and also the thoughts of what is to come. When young people spend their youth in sin and vanity, it gives them no pleasure but in what is present; it has a tendency to make the prospect of that which is future uncomfortable and terrible. And therefore such young people are not wont to think much of what is future; such thoughts are very disagreeable to them, so that they do what they can to shut them out of their minds. But when young people walk in ways of virtue and Christianity it not only gives them abundantly the most pleasant enjoyment of the present time, but renders the prospect of what is to come exceedingly comfortable and joyful.

They who spend their youth in the excerise of true religion may think of old age with comfort. If they should live to it, they may have reasonable comfort in all the changes of it, and have just cause to think of death with comfort. Such persons may think of eternity with unspeakable joy. We are born for an eternal duration; those who are now young have had their beings but a little while, and they will have those beings to all eternity. Religion will give rational comfort and joy; let them look as far forward as they will in this endless duration. And those things that are most terrible to wicked young people, that is, death, judgment, and eternity, may well be and often are the most comfortable and joyful of all things to them.

Application

I would improve this doctrine earnestly to exhort young people to embrace religion and virtue, and to walk in the ways thereof. I am confident that there are none of you, if you have given attention to what I have said and considered it as I went along, but that your reason has given its suffrage to the truth of it. If you haven't yet made trial, and so have never experienced the pleasures of a life of piety, yet, if you have seriously thought of the matter, you can't but conclude that it must be the most comfortable and pleasant life.

I dare appeal to the most vicious youth in the congregation, or other persons who are past their youth and have spent it in vice: if they give their judgment with consideration, whether or not you can judge that you have enjoyed yourself the better and have had more comfort in the world than you would have had if you had walked in virtuous ways and had ever been strict to the rules of virtue.

Let me therefore earnestly exhort you to forsake all ways of vice and youthful vanity, to renounce all licentious practices and sinful indulgences of carnal appetites, not to employ your mind when you are alone in vain imaginations and sinful thoughts; but let the time be filled up with serious and religious meditations of God, the condition of your precious souls, and of the great things of an approaching eternity.

Be exhorted to forsake all vanity and licentiousness in company, to avoid lewd ways of using your tongue, and not to employ it to the purposes of uncleanness or irreligion.

Forsake wicked companions if you see that they won't reform with you. Resolve for the time to come that all your behavior and all your diversions shall be governed by the rules of virtue and Christianity.

Be exhorted to forsake all those ways that have a tendency to prevent or hinder the flourishing of religion and the efficacy of the Word and ordinances in your souls.

I would on this occasion renewedly exhort and press you not to make it your practice to go immediately from the public worship and hearing of the Word into company, nor to make Sabbath days and lecture days your times of company-keeping and merriment .

Let me entreat you to continue in that reformation which I hope many of you have begun in this particular. I hope you are generally convinced of the reasonableness of it, and that experience has or will convince you that there is no great difficulty in it and that there is no danger of your sustaining any loss by it, or that your youth will be the less pleasant for it.

Earnestly seek that you may have the gracious presence of God and His smiles, a good conscience, and a sense of God's favor accompanying the pleasure that you have in outward things, which will unspeakably sweeten them. Seek that divine grace in your heart whereby your soul may be beautified, adorned, and rendered lovely in the eyes of God, and whereby you may live a life of divine love, a life of love to Christ and communion with Him. And see that you may have spiritual and heavenly appetites, and that you may be fitted for those noble and excellent pleasures of which you have now heard. Seek the great privilege of having a conversation in heaven and an intercourse with God and the blessed Jesus, instead of vain and lewd earthly companions.

Be exhorted, if you would live a pleasant life here and would be happy forever, to apply yourself with all your might to seek these things. I will here mention two things further to enforce this exhortation:

First, by this doctrine, one of the greatest objections of young people against religion is cut off. This is a main thing that hinders young people from embracing the ways of religion: they are in pursuit of their pleasures. This is what they aim at: to spend their youth pleasantly. And they think that if they forsake sin and youthful vanity, and take upon themselves a religious course of life, it will hinder them in their pursuit. They look upon religion as a very dull, melancholy thing and think that, if they embrace it, they will, in a great measure, be done with pleasures.

But what has now been offered to you shows the fallaciousness of such an objection, and shows that religion, instead of being a hindrance to your spending youth pleasantly, will be the most direct way to it, and indeed is the only way. The pleasantness of no other kind of life is worthy to be compared to it.

This is in addition to all manner of other reasons why you should embrace religion. 'Tis certain that a re-

ligious and holy life has the greatest excellency to recommend it. 'Tis fit in itself that you should embrace it
for the excellency of it alone, for 'tis that that makes
persons heavenly and confirms them to God. You are
under the strongest obligations in duty to do so; the
obligations are infinitely great.

You will deserve an infinite punishment if you do
not; you will rebel against the God who made you, and
"in whose hand your breath is and whose are all thy
ways."

You can't answer the end of your being if you don't.
Walking in the ways of religion and virtue would be infinitely profitable; thereby you would obtain eternal life
and glory in heaven. You are under the most extreme
necessity of embracing the ways of virtue and religion.
If you don't, God will be your eternal Enemy, and you
will perish forever and ever.

You are under the greatest obligation to spend your
youth in religion, for it is very uncertain whether you
will ever have any other opportunity, whether you won't
die in your youth. And if you should live till you are old,
if you don't turn to God in youth, it is very uncertain
whether ever you will. So it would be the greatest folly
not to improve your youth in religion, if a religious life
were never so unpleasant. But when you consider all
these things, 'tis the most direct course to live a pleasant life and to spend your youth pleasantly. Certainly it
will be a folly that wants a name and can't be expressed
if you refuse it and still spend your youth in sin and
vanity.

All these things are in addition to the inducement
the doctrine affords. How great indeed will be your folly
if you still go obstinately on.

If there is any one young person brought to any seriousness by what has been said, I would counsel such a
one to hearken to these articles of advice:

First, make no delay. Early youth is the best opportunity. It grows worse if you delay; there is no probability of improving the first motions of the Spirit of God.

Second, thoroughly consider the matter and come to some full determination of mind. Don't halt between two opinions, but be like Moses or like David.

Third, settle it with yourself that the business of religion will be attended to no purpose unless you are thoroughly devoted to it. Do not only seek, but strive; suffer violence. Christ has sufficiently forewarned us. He told us to cut off our right hands if necessary, and to sell all.

Fourth, when you have begun, hold on and hold out to the end. Proverbs 14:14: "The backslider in heart shall be filled with his own ways." Luke 9:62: "No man, having set his hand to the plow and looking back is fit for the kingdom of God." Hosea 6:3: "Then shall we know if we follow on."

I shall conclude with Proverbs 8:34: "Blessed is the man that heareth me, watching daily at my gates, waiting at the posts of my doors."

6

God Is Very Angry at the Sins of Children

(To the children at a private meeting
February 1740/41)

"And he went up from thence unto Bethel, and as he was going up by the way there came forth little children out of the city, and mocked him, and said unto him, 'Go up, thou bald head; go up, thou bald head.' And he turned back and looked on them, and cursed them in the name of the LORD. And there came forth two she bears out of the wood, and tare forty and two children of them." 2 Kings 2:23-24

Observe who they were who were here spoken of: they were children.

Observe the sin they were guilty of: they carried themselves contemptuously and proudly towards Elisha, a holy man and a prophet of God, as he was going by the way. The children who were playing in the streets, instead of paying respect to him and doing him reverence as he went along, mocked him, saying, "Go up, thou bald head; go up, thou bald head."

Observe how they brought the curse of God upon themselves by it.

Observe the dreadful effect of God's anger and curse.

DOCTRINE: God is very angry at the sins of children.

1. I would observe that children are guilty of a great

56

deal of sin. Persons are guilty of a great deal of sin while they are children.

Their hearts are naturally full of sin. They aren't naturally inclined to God, and they have no love for God. They have no delight in religion; they hate God's ways regarding Sabbaths and prayer; they naturally don't mind what God says to them; they are naturally senseless, proud, full of malice and hatred, inclined to wicked thoughts, and they have nothing good in them. Psalm 58:3: "The wicked are estranged from the womb; they go astray as soon as they be born, speaking lies."

They commit an abundance of actual sins. They live in neglect of God and are regardless of Him; they live in the neglect of Christ without any love for Him. They commit an abundance of sin on Sabbath days and in times of the worship of God. They disobey God by not seeking their salvation. They have wicked thoughts and wicked desires, and they tell many lies, which is a sin that is dreadfully threatened in Revelation 21:8: "All liars shall have their part in the lake which burneth with fire and brimstone. . . ."

They are guilty of unsuitable carriage to parents. They hate their parents, hate one another, and they quarrel, even with their own brothers and sisters. There are multitudes of kinds of wickedness that children are guilty of. They serve the devil and behave themselves like the devil's children.

2. God is very angry with them for their sins. He is very angry to see their hearts so full of sin, to see them of such a wicked disposition. He hates to see it; it is loathsome to Him and abominable in His sight.

He is not only angry enough to correct them, but to cast them into hell to all eternity. They deserve to burn in hell forever.

Their being children doesn't excuse them. Though they do not have so much knowledge, yet they know better, especially those children who live under the light of the gospel. Wicked children are in God's sight like young serpents. Now we hate young snakes.

They are the children of the devil. And as God hates the devil, so He abhors his children. The devil is the old serpent, and wicked children are his children.

Though children do not have as much knowledge, so neither do they have so many temptations as grown persons.

God is angry with them because they give the first part of their lives to the devil. When God has but lately made them, they take themselves away from God and give themselves to the devil.

God is so angry that He sends many children to hell for those things. Many times He won't allow them to live till they grow up. He cuts them off while they are children. So angry is He at the sins of children that He won't allow the earth to bear them. If they serve the devil, the devil shall have them.

God is so angry with them that if they never are converted God will surely punish them. Though they should live to be old, God will never forget the sins they are guilty of when they are children.

Application

USE OF EXHORTATION. Let this exhort you children who are here present to seek that you may be converted and get an interest in Christ so that your sins may be forgiven.

All of you have precious souls. Had I not known that, I would not have called you together today. You are all naturally in a miserable state and condition, and in a little time you will be in eternity, some sooner and some later.

Therefore now consider what you have been told and have heard of the anger of God at the sins of children. Consider what sinful creatures you are; therefore, you who are out of Christ, God is angry with you every day. How dreadful is that, to have God so angry with you?

There is no other way to be delivered but by Christ. Therefore seek an interest in Him. Consider that you can't bear the wrath of God. You cannot endure eternal burnings. How dreadful will it be to be in hellfire amongst devils, and know that you must be there to all eternity? God will have no mercy upon you. If you cry to Him, He won't hear you.

Consider how it will be when you come to die and are unconverted.

Consider how it will be at the day of judgment. Consider what you will see then.

You who are now mates together, who have often played together, who have gone to school together—how dreadful it will be to be separated then. How will you bear then to see some taken up into glory? And how dreadful will it be to be altogether in misery. Then you won't play together any more, but you'll be damned together. You will cry out with weeping and wailing and gnashing of teeth together. You will torment one another instead of playing together.

I hope that most of you have godly fathers and mothers who are concerned for the good of your souls, and who have often given you good counsel and have often prayed for you. How will you bear it at the day of judgment to see them?

If then you do not have an interest in Christ, your godly fathers and mothers will praise God for His justice in your damnation; they won't be grieved for you. Now they long for your salvation and are grieved for you. But then they will rise up and witness against you, and tell Christ how often they warned you.

All your godly neighbors will rise up and witness against you.

If you won't hearken to counsel, and so should die without an interest in Christ, your minister who now often preaches to you and warns you must rise up in judgment against you.

It is my duty now to earnestly seek your salvation. I am your pastor, and Christ has committed the care of your souls to me. Christ commands His ministers to feed the lambs of His flock.

But if you won't hearken, if you will not earnestly seek your salvation, but will spend away your time in sin, then I must rise up in judgment against you and declare to Christ how often I warned you. If you won't hearken, this very application will rise up in judgment against you.

But children who are converted will hereafter be a crown of joy and rejoicing to their faithful ministers in the day of judgment. How joyful would it be both to you and to me at the day of judgment if you might be my crown of rejoicing at the day of judgment. If you and I, who have been your minister and have preached to you and warned you, might stand together at that day in glory at Christ's right hand, so that I might say to Christ, "Here I am with the children which Thou hast given me."

How joyful that will be if you and your godly parents might meet in glory hereafter.

But if it should be otherwise, if you refuse to hearken to counsel and so should never get an interest in Christ and should therefore be at His left hand, turned into hell with devils, how you will cry out of your foolishness and say, "Oh, that I should be such a fool!" How you will then remember this application.

I am concerned for you. I know you have precious

souls, and that as long as you are not converted you are everyday in danger of dropping into hell. I am afraid lest your soul should be lost.

I desire that every one of you may be saved. I desire that at the Day of Judgment you may all appear mounting up with wings, and not some of you rejoicing and others crying.

I am afraid lest the devil will beguile and deceive you, and destroy many of you—and that is the reason I have called you together at this time.

I know you will all die in a little time, though some sooner than others. It is not likely you will all live to grow up. Therefore now let me call upon you all to improve your time. Consider the good opportunity you now have. Proverbs 8:17: "They that seek Me early shall find Me."

It may be that some of you are under your first convictions. I would now invite you all to come to Christ. If you will come and give your hearts to Him, He is willing to receive you.

What a lovely sight it will be to see children, holy and devoted to Christ. What a pity it is that the beginning and morning of life should be given to the devil and spent in his service.

In some countries it is the custom for parents to offer up a great many of their children in sacrifice to the devil. Will you offer yourselves up in sacrifice to him?

If you obtain an interest in Christ, you will be happy children. Holy children are happy children.

Consider therefore what you will do. Will you hear Him? Will you set about your soul's concern in good earnest?

You have precious souls. Consider what you will do for them. Will you go away and serve the devil still, or will you hearken to Christ, and seek God and your own salvation?

Don't hearken to Satan, but hearken to Christ. And all of you, with one consent, improve the time of your youth to seek salvation.

Let those who have no hope of their being converted give themselves no rest till they have obtained some; and don't let them who have hope think that their work is done. And let all strive and press forward in ways of religion now. Don't backslide, but seek and work to the end. That will be the way to obtain a crown of life.

7

Children Ought to Love the Lord Jesus Christ above All Things in This World

(To the children, August 1740)

"He that loveth father or mother more than Me
is not worthy of Me." Matthew 10:37

It has often been so in the Christian church that some of the children in a family have professed the true religion and have loved Christ and yet their parents have been enemies to Christianity. So the children who were Christians must either renounce the Christian religion and cast off Christ, or they must forsake their parents and be cast off by them, turned out of doors, and be wholly denied the benefit of their parents' care, provision, and inheritance. Yea, sometimes parents have been so displeased with their children for following Christ that they have themselves delivered them up to death; they have had a hand in their being proceeded against by wicked rulers and so put to death.

There were many such instances especially in the first times of the gospel. This is what Christ speaks of in the two verses preceding our text: "For I am come to set a man at variance against his father and the daughter against her mother, and the daughter in law against her mother in law. And a man's foes shall be they of his own household." And therefore Christ says as He does in our text, "He that loveth father or mother more than

Me is not worthy of Me."

Christ would hereby give warning to such children as profess to be His followers, that if it should be that their parents should threaten to disinherit them and turn them out of doors, if they threaten to disown them or fail to treat them any more as their chidren, yea, if they should turn into enemies against them if they will not renounce Christ, I say, Christ warns them that if in such a case they showed more love to their families than to Him, and so forsake Him for fear of being cast off by their parents, He will renounce them at last as being not worthy to be owned as some of His.

DOCTRINE: Children ought to love the Lord Jesus Christ above all things in this world.

Though Christ says in the text that he who loves father or mother more than Him is not worthy to be His disciple, His words are not to be understood as being confined only to those who are in their childhood, or before they are grown up. Yet 'tis evident He has a special respect to children while they yet remain under their parents' roof and under their care, for He speaks of the division that shall be in households or families in the verse just before our text. He says that a man's foes shall be those of his own household. The words are especially accommodated to the state of children while in a state of childhood, when the affections of children are wont to be strongest towards their parents, as having not been so much conversant abroad among other objects as afterward.

Parents are very commonly the object of children's greatest affections while young. So the latter part of the verse, "he that loveth son or daughter more than Me," is epecially accommodated to the usual state of persons after they are grown, are out from under their parents' cover and have families of their own, when children are very commonly the dearest objects of their love.

The following reasons may be given why children ought to love Jesus Christ above all things in the world.

1. He is more lovely in Himself. He is one who is greater and higher than all the kings of the earth. He has more honor and majesty than they and yet He is innately good and full of mercy and love.

There is no love so great and so wonderful as that which is in the heart of Christ. He is one who delights in mercy. He is ready to pity those who are in suffering and sorrowful circumstances, one who delights in the happiness of His creatures. The love and grace that Christ has manifested as much exceeds all that which is is any in this world as the sun is brighter than a candle. Parents are often full of kindness towards their children, but that is no kindness like Jesus Christ's.

He is an infinitely holy One. He is God's holy child, so holy and pure that the heavens are not pure in His sight; so holy that He is fairer than the sons of men, as the psalmist says in Psalm 45:2. Song of Solomon 5:10 says that He is the fairest among ten thousand, altogether lovely because of His glorious excellency. He is compared to the sun, that is the brightest of all things that we behold with our bodily eyes. He is called the sun of righteousness in Malachi 4:2, and He is called the morning star, the brightest of all the whole multitude of stars, in Revelation 22:16.

He is so lovely and excellent that the angels in heaven greatly love Him; their hearts overflow with love for Him, and they are continually day and night without ceasing praising Him and giving Him glory. Yea, He is so lovely a Person that God the Father infinitely delights in Him. He is His beloved Son, the brightness of His glory, whose beauty God continually sees with infinite delight without ever being weary of beholding it. Proverbs 8:30: "I was daily His delight, rejoicing always before Him." If the angels and God Himself love Him so much above all, surely children ought to love Him above all things in this world.

Everything that is lovely in God is in Him, and everything that is or can be lovely in any man is in Him; for He is man as well as God. He is the holiest, meekest, most humble, and in every way the most excellent man who ever was.

He is the delight of heaven; there is nothing in heaven, that glorious world, that is brighter, more amiable and lovely than Christ. This darling of heaven became a man, becoming as a plant or flower springing out of the earth; and He is the most lovely flower that ever was seen in this world. In Song of Solomon 2:1 it is said of Christ, "I am the Rose of Sharon, and the lily of the valleys."

2. There is more good to be enjoyed in Him than in everything or in all things in this world. He is not only an amiable good, but an all-sufficient good. There is enough in Him to answer all our wants and to satisfy all our desires. Children, if they come to Christ and set their hearts on Him, will find in Him that which is better for them and will be sweeter to them than anything that is to be had in the presence and company or provision of their parents, and better than anything that is to be found in their parents' houses.

Christ is the Bread of Life; in Him their souls may feed and feast upon that which will be much better than anything they are ever fed with at their fathers' tables.

Christ is to those who love Him as glorious clothing and excellent ornaments to their souls. These children who love Him, their souls are clothed with those robes that are a thousand times more beautiful and desirable than the best clothing their parents can provide for them. In Him they shall have that good which will be as gold tried in the fire that will make them richer than if they were king's children.

Christ is the most suitable good for them; if they love Him they will find Him sweeter to them than the honey and the honeycomb. In Him they shall find enough, all that they desire, and He will give them rest and satisfaction.

3. Christ has a higher right to children than any in this world. Their parents have a right to them, but Christ has a higher right, for He has made them. They are under greater obligations to give Christ their hearts and devote their whole souls to Him than to any other, for He has given them their souls and made them capable of knowing more about God and Christ than the beasts to the end that they might love Him.

And besides, the children of Christian parents have been given up to Christ in their baptism; and if they therefore don't give themselves to Christ with all their hearts, and don't love Him above all, they will violate what was done in their baptism. They have been as really given up to God as Samuel was by his mother, who gave him to the Lord all the days of his life and brought him when he was but a child to the tabernacle to live there (though they haven't been given in just the same manner).

There are many poor children in the world who are brought by their parents and offered up to idols and devils, and are burned alive as a sacrifice to them. Children among us, through God's great goodness to them, are not dealt with with such cruelty, but are offered up to Christ in baptism so that when they become capable of it they may offer their hearts up as a sacrifice to Christ by their great love for Him.

4. Children ought to love Christ above all in that He has done more for them than all the men in the world have ever done. Their parents have done a great deal for them; they have suffered a great deal for them, espe-

cially their mothers. And both their fathers and mothers have done a great deal in taking care of them, in providing for them, and bringing them up. They have been at a great deal of pains and cost for them.

But they have never done as much for them as Christ has done; for it is Christ who has kept them all their lives long. He has kept them from death. He has healed them when they have been sick, and they have always lived upon the provision that Christ has made for them. It has been through the hands of their parents, but their parents could not have given to them had not Christ provided it for them. They have always lived upon Christ's provision: He has maintained them, and it is His wool and His flax that has clothed them. If it had not been for Christ's preservation they would have been in the grave, and there they would have been eaten up by worms long ago.

It is Christ who has kept them out of the hands of the devil. The devil, if Christ permitted, would immediately fall upon and carry them away. It is Christ who has kept them out of hell. If it had not been for Christ, they would have been burning in hell among devils long before this time. It is He who keeps them every night while they sleep. And, which is more than all, Christ has died for children. None can conceive what dreadful things Christ has suffered, and all this He suffered not only for grown persons but for children. All children are by nature children of wrath and are in danger of eternal damnation in hell. But children who live under the gospel have an opportunity to be delivered from hell, to become the children of God, and so to go to heaven when they die. Therefore they have the opportunity to be happy and to shine forth as the sun in the kingdom of God, and enjoy rivers of pleasures at God's right hand forevermore.

This opportunity they have by the blood of Christ;

they could have had no such opportunity but by its costing Christ His life and His undergoing great cruelties and a very tormenting death, though He was God's only Son.

Nowhere in this world is there anyone who has done so much for children as this. Where is anything that any have done for them to be compared with this? Surely then they ought to love Christ more than all things in this world.

5. Never has anyone in this world showed such wonderful condescension in taking notice of children and offering Himself to them and seeking their love as Christ has done. If some great king should occasionally pass through a town, and should take much notice of children and show great affection and kindness to them, would not this be wonderful! But this would not be as wonderful as that Christ, who is the King of Heaven and the King of Kings should take gracious notice of them. But this is what Christ does: He graciously offers Himself and all the great blessings that He has purchased by His death to them. He is willing to be theirs so that they may say of this glorious King, "This is Jesus, my Friend; this is my Redeemer, my Portion, one who has given Himself to me."

That is the voice of Christ in Proverbs 8:32: "Now therefore hearken unto Me, O ye children." And Psalm 34:11: "Come, ye children, hearken unto Me."

When Christ was upon earth and they were about to bring little children to Him that he might bless them, others rebuked them; they thought it was too much for them to expect that so great a Person as Christ should take notice of little children. Christ frowned upon them who forbade it and said, "Suffer the little children to come unto Me." He took them up in His arms and blessed them (Mark 10:13–16).

So He stands, as it were, with the arms of His love

open to receive all children: He would have them come
to Him that He may bless them. He won't despise their
love. He is willing to accept it and to give them sweet
manifestations of His love for them.

It would be a great thing for some great man to enter into communion with some poor child; but Christ
is ready to receive little children into communion with
Himself. Even the poorest of children of the poorest of
parents, those who are despised in this world, Christ
doesn't despise them.

He doesn't only offer to give Himself to children,
but to give them His kingdom, to give them all that He
has, and to give them His angels so that they shall be
their angels, though they are glorious creatures.

Christ is very angry with any who despise one little
child who believes in Him. Christ says in Matthew
18:10: "Take heed that ye despise not one of these little
ones; for I say unto you that in heaven their angels do
always behold the face of My Father which is in
heaven."

Thus wonderfully does Christ condescend to children. He stands, as it were, at their door and knocks,
and says to them, "If you hear My voice, I will come in
and eat with you."

Application

1. This first use may be of conviction, to convince
those children who have no true love to the Lord Jesus
Christ of their sin and misery. Are there not many of
you here present who have never truly loved the Lord
Jesus Christ? Though He is so excellent a Person,
though you have often heard of Him, though He has
done so much for you, though you have heard often
how much He has suffered for you, though you have

been given up to Christ in your baptism and been so greatly distinguished from other poor, miserable children who have been offered up to the devil, though Christ condescends to offer Himself to you, though you have heard the gospel preached and been taught so much at home and at meetings, yet you have never truly loved Him.

Don't flatter yourselves that you love Christ when you don't. Consider whether it doesn't appear that many of you have never loved Him by your living such a life as you have done. If you had loved Christ, would you have been so careless of doing the things that He has commanded you? Would you not have been more careful not to sin against Him? Would you have spent away your time in thinking so little of Christ? Persons are apt to think much of those whom they love. Would you have spent your time in thinking so little of Him, and of nothing but your play and the vanities of this world? Would you not have loved the Word of Christ? Would you not have loved Christ's holy day? The Sabbath day is Christ's day.

Have you loved Christ's house? Would you have cried in the neglect of secret prayers? 'Tis to be feared that many of you who can pray have lived very much without going to Christ alone to pray to Him, to God the Father, who are both one God. If you loved Christ, you would love to go to Him in prayer. Many of you have hearkened to the devil more than to Christ, for when you have done wickedly in telling lies and disobeying your parents, in giving way to a spirit of hatred to others, and in breaking the Sabbath day, then you have hearkened to the devil.

It is to be feared that many of you children who are here have never had the least spark of true love for Christ in your hearts since you were born. If it is thus with you, this may convince you of the following:

First, how angry God is with you. God is very angry with those who don't love Christ. He is God's own dear son. God knows that He is infinitely lovely. God is angry when He sees that persons who hear how much Christ has done for them and yet have no love for Him. 1 Corinthians 16:22: "If any man love not the Lord Jesus Christ, let him be anathema maranatha," that is, let him be an accursed creature. So if you don't love Christ you are under God's curse; and if you never love Him you will be a cursed, miserable creature forever. Is it any wonder that such a curse is denounced against those who contend with God?

Second, this may convince you that you can't desire that Christ should have any respect to you by anything that you do. You have sinned greatly against Him in that you have not loved Him, that you have continued so long without any love to Him, and have been guilty of disobeying His commands. How can such a sinful creature ever deserve that Christ should love Him? You don't at all deserve that Christ should look upon you. You deserve that He should hate you all the days of your life, and that He should cast you into hell forever. You deserve that He should loath all your prayers and all the best that you can do.

Let you do what you will for your own salvation, yet how can you deserve that God should have mercy upon you when you do what you do not from love to Christ, but only from love to yourself?

Third, this may convince you that you can't be saved in any other way than by the blood of Christ. It shows that you can't be saved by your own righteousness, for you are so sinful and wicked a creature that none of your righteousness is worthy to be accepted. You need Christ's blood to wash away your sins, to cleanse you from the guilt of not loving Christ, and from all your disobedience to Him. You are so wicked that God will never accept you in any other way. He won't save you on any other account but only for Christ's sake, His own dear Son who has died for poor sinners.

Therefore, when you pray to God to save you, you must not expect that God will ever do it unless it is for Christ's righteousness, and not for yours. He will never hear your prayers unless it is out of respect to Christ. Therefore don't expect to be heard in any other way. If you could pray every day, as long as you live, and spend most of your time in reading, praying, and crying in sorrow for your sins, yet all this would be nothing. It won't make up for your sins. But Christ has made up for sin, and therefore if ever God hears your prayers, makes you His child, and saves you from hell, it will be for Christ's sake alone—not because you took so many pains in reading, praying, and doing your duty, but because of what Christ did for poor sinners.

2. This second use may be of exhortation to children to seek earnestly that they may be converted, and that God would fill their hearts with love for Christ now while they are young. But if you should die while you are young and death should come upon you and find you without any love for Christ, what will become of you? How uncertain it is whether you will live another day. What multitudes die while they are but children. How do you know but that some dreadful distemper will overtake you? How dreadful it will be to you on your deathbed without any love for Christ, and what will become of your poor soul when you are dead?

If you truly love Christ above all, you shall enjoy His love to you. See what Christ has said in Proverbs 8:17: "I love them that love Me." In those words Christ has a special respect to children and young persons, as appears by the next words: "And those that seek Me early shall find Me." How blessed and happy is that child whom the great King of Heaven, angels, and men love.

If you truly love Christ, all the glorious angels of heaven will love you, for they delight in those who love Christ; they love to see such a sight as children giving their hearts to Christ. There will be joy in heaven among the angels. The day that you begin to love Christ, the angels will be your angels; they will take care of you while you sleep. God will give them charge to keep you in all your ways, and they will do it with delight because they will love you.

If you sincerely love Jesus Christ, it will be the way for you to live a comfortable, pleasant life, then you may have peace in your own mind and may live without fear. When other children who don't love Christ are afraid of dying, because they are afraid they shall go to hell when they die, you need not be afraid. Then you need not be afraid of thunder, which is commonly very terrifying to children. Consider that it is your Father and your Redeemer who thunders; the thunder is His voice. Thunder and lightning can never do them any hurt who love Christ, for if they are taken out of the world by it, yet it only carries them from this world to heaven into the glorious presence of Christ.

It is sweet to the soul to love Christ; it is a holy affection that fills the soul with sweetness. Then you will have the pleasure of living a life of communion with Christ, which will be a very sweet life.

If you love Christ above all it will tend to make you love everybody, which will greatly benefit your life. How much better will you live if you live in love more than if you live in strife and jarring with one another?

If you love Christ, you will be safe from the devil, that roaring lion that goes about seeking whom he may devour. He will not be able to hurt you, for you shall be out of his reach. If the devil should appear to you, you need not be afraid of him, but may triumph over him. The devil knows that Christ will subdue him under the feet of such as love Him. Christ will bring down that dreadful giant and cause all holy children who love Him to come and set their feet upon the devil's neck.

If you love the Lord Jesus Christ, it will have a tendency to make the Sabbath day a pleasant day to you.

If you have the holy principle of love to Christ in your heart, you will be fit to live in the world; you can't be fit to live without that, for they who have no love for Christ, if they do live, they'll only live in sin and in the service of Satan. But they who love Christ will live for the glory of God and will have God's blessing upon them in the convoys of life.

If you love Christ, you will be fit to die. When you die you will die safely and will have good ground of comfort. When you die, Christ, whom you have loved, will receive your departing spirit; you will be welcomed into heaven by your dear Savior and by all those glorious saints and angels who attend Him.

There are glorious promises that Christ has made to those who love Him. He has promised them a crown of life (James 1:12). And when you come to die, then that glorious crown shall be set upon your head, which will be a thousand times more excellent than the best crown that is worn by any king or queen.

If you should die in your childhood, how comfortable would it be to your parents if they had any comfortable evidences of your having truly loved Christ? If they are bereaved of you by death, it will doubtless leave them very mournful and sorrowful; and if you gave no hopeful testimonies of being saved, that will be the sting of their sorrow. They will be afraid that your poor soul is burning in hell.

But if you love Jesus Christ, they can with comfortable hope think of your soul as being with Him in glory in a joyful, blessed state. And that will be the best comfort in their sorrow; it will greatly support their hearts while your dead body lies in its grave.

If you should not die in childhood, yet, if you don't love Christ while you are young, your hearts will grow hard.

Consider further how many have truly loved Christ while they are young. Let the wonderful work of God on children in other places stir you up to earnestly seek God so that you may partake of the same blessing.

Pray earnestly to God to give you true love for Christ. Your heart is wholly full of love for sin and enmity against Christ; you can't work love for Christ in your own heart. Cry to God to draw your heart to Christ. John 6:44: "No man can can come to the Son unless the Father draw him."

Avoid those things that Christ hates. If you do those things that He hates, it will tend to make you hate Christ more and more.

Be very earnest in this matter. Remember the exhortation now given. Don't only seek a little while; that is not the way to obtain. Hosea 6:3: "Then shall we know, if we follow on to know the Lord."

8

Corrupt Communication

(For a meeting of the young people, July 1740)

"Let no corrupt communication proceed out of your
mouth, but that which is good to the use of edifying,
that it may minister grace unto the hearers."
Ephesians 4:29

The words contain a precept and counsel from an
exhortation of the apostle to the Christian Ephesians
respecting their speech or discourse one with another.
The exhortation consists of two parts:

1. A declaration wherein he advises against something: "Let no corrupt communication proceed out of
your mouth," in which may be observed two things:
First, the thing dehorted from or advised against: corrupt communication. The word in the original translated "corrupt" properly signifies rotten as the flesh of a
noisesome sore or as the flesh of a rotten, stinking carcass. This intimates that such kind of communication
as often proceeds out of the mouths of wicked men is
foul and filthy, more loathsome than the corruption of
a stinking wound or than the rotten flesh of carrion,
which men would abhor to have in their mouths. Much
more should they abhor to have such corrupt, filthy
talk in their mouths as wicked men sometimes have.

Second, we may observe the manner in which the
apostle advises against it: "don't let it proceed out of
your mouth," that is, utterly avoid it. Never be guilty of
it; do not let your conscience have reason to accuse you

of it; never let any such words come forth out of your mouth. The mouth is a part of our bodies into which we abhor to have that which is outwardly corrupt, such as stinking flesh, enter; but much more should we abhor to have that which is morally corrupt and filthy proceed out of our mouths, for not that which goes into the mouth, but that which comes out of the mouth defiles the man (Matthew 15:11).

2. The other part of the advice that the apostle here gives is an exhortation wherein something is exhorted to, wherein may be observed two things: first, the thing advised, which is virtuous and profitable discourse. There are two phrases used: that which is good to the use of edifying, that is, that which is good in itself and tends to do good to others, such discourse whereby you promote the good of each other's souls.

Second, the good end and great benefit of such discourse with which the apostle enforces this advice: "That it may minister grace to the hearer." Such discourse tends to the best and most excellent benefit of those who hear it; it tends to minister grace to them, which is the most excellent benefit than any can receive, and is a thousand times better than if it ministered silver and gold, earthly pleasures, temporal health, or any other good whatsoever.

DOCTRINE: Professing Christians, when they meet together, should avoid all corrupt discourse one with another, and should practice that whereby they may promote the good of each other's souls.

They should avoid all corrupt communication or discourse. Particularly:

1. They should avoid all profane conversation, all speaking lightly of those things that are of a sacred and divine nature. This is what many persons, especially young persons, are prone to. In a corrupt time, being of a serious and solemn spirit, and showing a great regard

to things of religion is out of credit among young people; and those who appear to be of such a spirit will be called "precise" and will be charged with being needlessly and foolishly scrupulous. Very often they will be charged with being hypocrites, being proud of their religion, and of having a mind to appear better than others.

On the contrary, they are ready to look upon their godly conversation as something credible, and what will recommend them to their companions who speak of the things of religion only to make jest of them, or at least to speak lightly of such things with a jesting air.

Such conversation is very corrupt and very provoking to God. It is more fit for heathens than for Christians. To speak lightly of things of religion is to speak lightly of God and to condemn Him, and is so looked upon by God.

2. Professing Christians should avoid all unclean or lascivious communication. There are many persons, especially young persons, who are full of such conversation as this; they are foul-mouthed persons and seem to delight in unclean kinds of songs, telling lascivious stories, and in talking with a bold air about those things that modesty forbids to mention. They seem to look upon it as their honor that they dare break rules of modesty in their talk, as if it was a great attainment, a very commendable courage, to show that they aren't afraid to speak those things that modest persons choose to avoid mentioning.

With many young people, he is the best man who shows most of that kind of boldness, wit, and courage; who appears in unclean, lascivious talk and jesting. Their diversion consists very much in such kind of mirth.

This is exceedingly unbecoming a Christian. Such persons, however much they may value themselves on their impudence and unclean wit, appear more like brute beasts than Christians. True Christianity is as abhorrent to any such thing as light is to darkness, and the exercise of Christian holiness will make men to more abhor to take such unclean words and talk into their mouths than they would abhor to take a piece of a dead, rotten carcass crawling full of worms into their mouths. The apostle advises that such unclean communication is not so much as once to be named among Christians. Ephesians 5:3: "But fornication and all uncleanness and covetousness, let it not be once named among you as becometh saints, neither filthiness nor foolish talking nor jesting, which are not convenient." This requires Christians, whose bodies are the temples of God and who are persons devoted to the holy Jesus, to be pure in heart and mouth. They should follow after whatsoever things are pure (Philippians 4:8). Christians are the children of the light and of the day, and therefore should walk as children of the light (Romans 13:13). Let us walk honestly as in the day, not in chambering and wantonness. Christians are advised by the apostle in Colossians 3:5–8 to put away all filthy communication out of their mouths, and advises again in Colossians 4:6 that their speech should always be with grace and seasoned with salt. Salt is used to preserve meat from putrefying and becoming rotten carrion, as otherwise it would do. So our words should be kept from uncleanness, which makes them like filthy, noisesome corruption.

3. Another sort of corrupt discourse that Christians should avoid when they meet together is talking against others. A great part of the conversation of many young people when they get together consists in making themselves diversion with others' faults and blemishes. Very much of the mirth and laughter that young people have together consists in making talking and

laughing at these and those things that others who are absent have said and done.

Many seem to take pride in speaking of others behind their backs with an air of contempt, and make sport of the those things in them that they reckon show how weak and foolish they are. They spend a great deal of time talking against other young people, and also ridiculing old people; and so they entertain one another and pass away the time that they spend together. This is very unbecoming professing Christians. A great many stories are told against others; many false and slanderous reports are told, and things are set out beyond the truth to make others appear more ridiculous, and to make more sport for themselves, which is very unbecoming professing Christians. When it is inquired in Psalm 15:1, "Who shall abide . . . ?" it is answered in verse 3, "he that backbiteth not with his tongue." Psalm 101:5 says, "Whosoever privily slandereth his neighbor will I cut off." The apostle advises in Ephesians 4:31 that all evil speaking be put away from among Christians, and so does the Apostle Peter in 1 Peter 2:2. The Apostle James particularly warns Christians against this in James 4:11: "Speak not evil one of another brethren. He that speaketh evil of his brother . . . ."

Another sort of discourse that may be called corrupt and that professing Christians should avoid is that which is unseasonable or unsuitable for the time. When persons are together on the Sabbath, they will talk of worldly and indifferent matters; they use diverting kinds of discourse or talk of worldly and indifferent matters as they do on other days. Such talk as at another time may be innocent may become very corrupt by its unseasonableness.

So persons will, as it were, mix religion and vain and diverting discourse, such as when persons come together under pretense of holding a religious meeting for reading and praying, and such religious exercises, and will immediately, as soon as the religious exercise is over, fall into loose diverting to jesting and laughing, or go into vain diverting talk, manifesting that they have attended religion merely out of custom; showing that they have done it as a task and are glad it is over. They are willing to get as far from it as ever they can. This is but to make a mockery of duties of religion. When religious meetings are attended after this manner, it would be better if they were not attended at all. When things are thus disagreeably mixed together, it renders both their religious exercise and their discourse too abominable to God. This is something like the Jews bringing their sheep, oxen, doves, and worldly concerns into the temple, at which Christ expressed so much indignation.

The second point in our text is that when Christians meet together they should use such discourse as may be profitable and whereby they may promote the good of each others' souls.

1. They should use such discourse as is innocent and virtuous, agreeable to the rule of God's Words, watching diligently over their mouth and setting a watch upon the door of their lips. Psalm 141:3: "Set a watch, O Lord, before my mouth. Keep the door of my lips." Psalm 39:1: "I said I will take heed to my ways. I will keep my mouth with a bridle." Christians are to use their tongues for the glory of God and as becomes reasonable creatures. Christians are to avoid all appearance of profaneness, in all foolish talking and jesting, all backbiting, being blameless and harmless, as the sons of God, being pure and honorable in their conversation.

2. They should accustom themselves to such conver-

sation as may tend to each other's instruction and growth in Christian knowledge, knowledge of the things of God. They should discourse of the doctrines and principles of religion, inquiring one of another, and entering into such discourse as tends to enlightening one another. They should discourse about the Word of God, of things that are contained in the Holy Scriptures, engaging one another in reading and searching the Scriptures, and helping each other to understand the meaning of it. They should be discoursing together of things that they hear in the preaching of the Word, which would be an excellent means of fastening things that they hear in their memory and engaging their attention more in hearing for the time to come. This would also cause the preaching of the Word to make a greater impression on their minds, and would prevent their hearing all only in a customary, slight manner, losing all as soon as they come out of the meetinghouse.

They should discourse together on the works and the attributes of God, His power and wisdom in creation, in His providence and, above all, in the work of redemption. Psalm 105:2: "Talk ye of all His wondrous works." Psalm 145:10–12: "All thy works shall praise Thee, O LORD, and Thy saints shall bless Thee. They shall speak of the glory of Thy kingdom, and talk of Thy power; to make known to the sons of men His mighty acts, and the glorious majesty of His kingdom." This that is here spoken of as the practice of the saints is an excellent practice most becoming the saints.

3. They should accustom themselves when together to talk of such things as tend to awaken and rouse each others' souls out of a careless, dull, and dead frame; and this may tend to beget in each other a deep sense of the infinite importance of the things of religion. They should speak much of the vanity of the things of

the world, the shortness and uncertainty of life, and how great a thing it is to die; they should be talking of the great things of another world, speaking of the day of judgment, the great things that will come to pass, of heaven and hell, talking much of eternity.

4. They should talk much of such things as tend to each other's warning. They should speak of the evil and danger of such and such sinful practices, the folly of ways, the corruption of the heart of man and its readiness to fall in with temptation, and the great need we stand in of divine help. They should particularly be speaking of the evil of such sins as persons of their age and circumstances are especially ready to fall into.

5. They should talk much of such things as have a tendency to kindle warm, holy affections in each others' souls. So they should talk much when together of Jesus Christ, His excellency, and the wonderful grace of God in giving Him to die for sinners; they should speak much of the dying love of Jesus Christ; they should speak much of the great benefits and blessings of the gospel that are bestowed on the saints, the glorious happiness of such as truly have an interest in Christ. They should speak much of the saints' happiness and glory in heaven, where they will be perfectly holy and happy in the full enjoyment of God and Christ, and where they will be in perfect love and friendship with another forever and ever. They should speak much of things that convey vital piety and the influence that the Holy Spirit of God has upon the souls of true saints, and of the exercises of the graces of the Holy Spirit.

6. They should be much in talking of such things as tend to direct and stir each other up to their duty. It should be a matter of discourse among them what their duty is in such and such cases, and of the difficulties and temptations that are commonly to be met with in the way of their duty, and of the need of divine help in

duty. They should be frequent in such discourse so that they may inure themselves to those temptations, and take heed that they keep their hand in it, if I may so speak, so that it may always be easy and natural to them to fall into such discourse. For the less they use themselves to it, the more difficulties will increase in the way of entering into it; and the more they accustom themselves to it, the more easy and pleasant will it be.

Application

The use that I would make of this doctrine is to exhort those here present, especially young persons, for whose sake this meeting was principally intended, to comply with the duty recommended in the doctrine. Let me now this day, whom God has set to be the watchman to watch for your souls, this day counsel and exhort you in the name of God to avoid all corrupt, vain, profane, unclean, and corrupt conversation. Accustom yourselves when with one another to such discourse as may be profitable, and by which you may promote the good of each others' souls. You are here this day to hear what counsels and direction I have to give you from the Word of God. And by coming here, you do, as it were, say that you desire to be instructed and directed in the way of your duty. You came for that end, and that you desire that I, who am your pastor, should tell you what you ought to do for your soul's good. And this is the advice that I have to give you, which you ought to receive as counsel from Christ Himself because it is agreeable to the mind and the Word of Christ, and that which certainly is wholesome for your soul.

I may expect that you will hearken to me because I know that many of you make a profession of loving God and Christ above all things in the world. I know that many of you have devoted yourselves to the service of God and the business of religion. Therefore let me pray you to hearken to some things that I have to say, to lay before you motives to stir you up to comply with this counsel, to accustom yourselves when together to such communication as has been spoken of.

1. Consider that the good of the soul is infinitely of the greatest concern.

2. Speech is one great thing whereby God has distinguished us from the brute creature and set us above them; and 'tis therefore most reasonable that we should improve it for Him.

3. Hereby you will promote your own and each other's profit and pleasure together. This will be the most profitable discourse. And, not only so, but you will find it to be the most pleasant. It would make your company and conversation much more pleasant than to fill it up with vanity, with foolish and lewd jesting, talking against others, spending away the time in that which serves no purpose but to take the heart off from everything that is good. Such conversation would be pleasant because it would be profitable; the profit that you would find in it would make you love it and take delight in it.

It would be pleasant because it would naturally tend to unite you in a virtuous friendship one with another. There is no discourse or conversation that so unites persons together as religious discourse, that by which they may instruct and profit each others' souls; it naturally tends to knit persons together in friendship. And the reason is that where such discourse is carried on, there the God of love and peace is present. There Christ is among them, the Prince of love and peace.

4. This is the way to keep a good conscience.

5. If you follow this advice, then your company won't

indispose you to the duty of secret prayer.

6. Then you will be in the way of the blessing of God in your company, and in all other concerns. See that blessed text of Scripture in Malachi 2:16–17.

7. Then you won't repent of your discourse and conversation afterwards. When you use corrupt discourse, vain and unclean speech, then you can expect to repent. You intend it.

8. This is the way not to lay a foundation in youth for calamities and sorrows all your life long. Job 13:26: "Thou writest bitter things against me. Thou makest me to possess the sins of my youth."

Seeing therefore that there are so many motives to induce you to hearken to this counsel, let me insist upon it with you who are here. When you come together, let Christ have a place among you; don't wholly shut Him out of your company. He is ready to be one of you. You aren't too good to admit Him into your company.

Yea, let me advise you to often take Him with you. He will do you no hurt in your company. He won't spoil it, but will make it in every way better, more profitable, more honorable, and more pleasant.

Is it not a great and infinite condescension in so glorious a Person that He will vouchsafe to be with you? Is His company not an unspeakable honor? If you will admit Christ, His love, His power, and His joy will be among you; those will spoil no company. And they will not only be with you then, but will follow you home and will remain with you oftentimes afterwards.

Be exhorted to make trial. You have heretofore used good and profitable speech. Why have you stopped? Did it do you any hurt? Did it spoil your company? Is it better with you since you stopped? Was God a wilderness to you, or a land of darkness that you have forsaken Him?

It may be that all who now hear me won't comply

with this exhortation; it may be that but a very few of this society will comply. I would therefore give advice in a few words to those few who are willing to hearken:

As much as you can, avoid the society of those who use corrupt communication and won't hearken to this warning.

Seek out company where profitable and religious discourses are used. Let those few who are willing associate together; if others mock and say that it is only pride and hypocrisy, don't regard them. God will observe it. God will hearken and hear, and a book of remembrance will be written.

See if you can find companions who will fall in with this advice, and then be much with them. And then Christ will be with you.

Let those whom you choose for your special, intimate friends be those who are lively in religion and who delight in religious conversation. Make those your special friends who may converse freely, without fear or suspicion of one another, without suspecting one another of pride and hypocrisy. And it is more natural for intimate friends to unburden themselves one to another.

After you have begun, take heed not to gradually leave off. Satan will envy your happiness. You have corruptions that will oppose you, and there will be many snares. But take heed of the beginnings. Keep up this practice with great care and watchfulness.

9

A Flower Cut Down

(To a private meeting of young people after Billy Sheldon's death February 1740/41 . Afterwards preached the doctrinal part with the new application at the end on the occasion of the death of my daughter Jerusha, February 21, 1747/8)

> "He cometh forth like a flower
> and is cut down." Job 14:2

In these words I would observe:

What man, with respect to his present life, is compared to a flower, a beautiful, pleasant part of the plant that most commonly is put forth in the spring in the most pleasant part of the year, and then appears fair and flourishing.

We may observe two things wherein he especially resembles this flower: in his beginning and end. In his beginning or his coming forth, he is like a flower in the spring of the year. It soon comes forth; in a day or two after it first begins to put forth, it appears in a full blossom.

So man comes forth quickly. He puts forth soon after he comes into the world; he grows up, comes on the stage of action, and begins to make a fair and promising appearance. He is a companion among young people; he is useful in the family to which he belongs and is taken notice of by others. He grows in stature, understanding, and action.

Man is like a flower in his end. He is cut down like

the flower that soon comes forth and is as soon gone as it came forth. In a day or two, it is gone. Presently, after the leaves of the flower are fully spread out, it falls. The wind blows it away from the trees. The flower that grows in the field, in the midst of its flourishing, in its most blooming state, is oftentimes cut down with one stroke of the scythe.

In speaking to these words I would:

1. Show how they are applicable to mankind in general.

2. Show how they are applicable to those who die in youth.

3. Show how they are applicable especially to those who die in youth, and then make some application.

1. It may well be said of all mankind that every man comes forth like a flower and is cut down. Man is a creature whom God has set in honor; he is, as it were, the flower of the lower creation. As the flower is, as it were, the crown of the plant on which it grows, so is man the crown of this lower world; he is fairest. God has given him a more comely and majestic aspect than the rest of the creatures. He has endowed him with excellent faculties of mind.

But when death soon comes and puts an end to his being in this world, it cuts down those flowers. However fair and flourishing he appeared for a while, he is cut down; and then he ceases anymore to make a figure in human society. There is an end put to him; however fair and comely in body he was, death mars his beauty, changes his countenance, and sends him away. However considerable he might be among men, death turns him to vile dust. However dear he was to his friends and relations, death soon takes him from among them and makes that alteration in him so that they desire to have him buried out of their sight.

When a person is dead, he never will be anymore in this world. He has gone where he shall not return. There is hope for a tree that is cut down that it may sprout again, and that the tender branch thereof will not cease. Though the roots thereof wax old in the earth and the stock thereof die in the ground, yet through the scant of water it may bud and bring forth boughs like a plant. But man dies and wastes away, yea, man gives up the ghost. And where is he, as the waters flow from the sea and the flood decays and dries up, so man lies down and does not rise again till the heavens are no more, as in verse 7 and following of our text. When he is dead, all his concern in this world is at an end.

This is especially to those who die in youth. A person in his youth may fitly be compared to a flower. As flowers mostly appear in the spring of the year, so when the year is in its beginning and all things are putting forth and growing, so youth is, as it were, the springtime season of life. The plant blossoms or bears its flower in its youth; as for those herbs or plants that are but of a year's continuance, the time of their flowering or blossoming is in their youth, or in the former part of their life. Toward the close of the year they are wont to bear seed. So youth is the flowering part of life.

The flower is the fairest and most beautiful part of the plant. The flower at first appears fresh and very lively, pleasing to the eye. The flower sends forth a pleasant fragrance.

So the time of youth is a time wherein human nature makes the fairest and most blooming appearance in many respects. The body then is in its greatest comeliness and activity then. Oftentimes persons appear as a pleasant flower: their faculties begin to bud forth, and they are pleasant to their parents and other relations, and they are pleasant among their companions.

When the plant is in bloom, the flower seems to rejoice. How the trees and the face of the earth in the spring, when covered with flowers, seem to be joyful.

So the time of youth is a time wherein persons are wont most to rejoice in the good things of the world. Then their spirits are most lively and their appetites strongest; then they have the greatest relish of the comforts and pleasures of this life; then they are usually most disposed to merriment, diversion, and pleasure.

The flower is a very promising part of the plant. It is not only in itself very fair and pleasant, but it promises fruit to succeed. When we see a tree full of flowers or blossoms, then we hope that it will bear well that year. So youth is an age wherein persons are commonly full of hopes and promises to themselves of the good and prosperity they shall see in the world. They are just entering upon the stage of the world and they promise themselves that they shall see and enjoy much afterwards. Others, such as their parents and friends, also are ready to promise them much future comfort and are full of hopes of seeing them settle, and oftentimes are full of hope of the figure they will make in the world.

A flower is a part of the plant that is of short continuance, very sudden in its growth; so it is with young persons: they have but very lately received an existence; they are, as it were, suddenly come forth and come upon the stage of the world.

2. When young people die, then the flower is cut down. A flower is a part of the plant that appears furthest from death, and yet is nearest to it. There is no part of the tree that appears so lively as the flower, and yet no part of it is so short-lived. How soon it vanishes; how soon the wind blows it away, and how quickly and suddenly the flowery growth of the field is mown down with the scythe.

This implies two things:

First, that death puts an end to all the pleasantness, that pleasing, promising appearance, and the being of young persons, and to all their concerns in the world.

Second, it does this sometimes suddenly. When the flower is cut down with a scythe, it falls at once. At one moment it stands in its flourishing, then in the next it is cut down. So it is, as it were, oftentimes with young people. How often they die without many days' warning; their death is unexpected; there is little time to think of death. Disease siezes upon them strongly, it baffles all medicines, and hastens them out of the world.

From what has been said, I would exhort and beseech the young people who are present to get ready for death. What you have now heard from the Word of God, you have lately seen verified in the providence of God. There have been several instances of it recently in the town. God tells you in His Word that man comes forth as a flower and is cut down. And He has not only told you so, but He has been showing you that it is so. He has cut down one flower after another of those who had but lately come forth, who were, as it were, just in the blossom. He has spoken not only once, but twice, yea, three times.

God is pleased to cut down some to warn others. He awfully takes some away by death so that others who survive may take warning, which is much more than if God only spoke in His Word to give you such warning. When God slays one to warn others, such a warning is a costly warning, and they are stupid who disregard it. It would be stupid hardness and provoking obstinacy in you to disregard one such warning, but God has renewed and multiplied His witnesses, and has called to you with so awful and solemn a voice again and again.

Besides the two instances of death in those who had just entered, as it were, upon their youth, God has now

very lately taken away one who was in the very morning
and blossom of his life, a very hopeful young man
whom you knew very well, whom you used to see often
at meetings, sitting there attending the public worship
of God, sitting to hear His Word. He was one whom you
saw very likely publicly presenting himself to solemnly
own his covenant and to stand with some others of you
in the house of God. Lately he sat with you at the Lord's
Table here; he was one whom you have often seen
about the town, and with whom many of you were acquainted. He often conversed with you, and has been a
companion to many of you. He was one who was a
pleasant flower, as it were, one who had just blossomed;
one who was a pleasant flower.

This flower, you see, is cut down and is withered and
gone. The place that has known him will know him no
more. Your eyes that have seen him will see him no
more in this world. He has gone into an eternal state
and condition.

He was young as many of you. He was in like circumstances with many of you. A little while ago he appeared as likely to live as you. When you lately saw him
at a meeting, he stood up to make open profession of
the Christian religion. He lately sat at the Lord's Table.
When he lately was in company with you, what was
there to show him to be nearer to death than you are?
What appearance was there of his being so near to
eternity? He did not know of it; none of his friends
knew anything of it; none of you could see any more
signs of approaching death in him than in yourself or
in others.

But now he is gone; this flower you lately saw flourishing in the morning and spring of life is cut down
and is not to be seen. You are yet spared; you as yet have
an opportunity to prepare for death. God has taken him
away, and it is God who has spared your lives. He has

taken him away to give you warning to prepare for death. God in this instance has shown you what you must be the subject of ere long. He has shown you that you don't know how soon you may die. He has shown you that you don't know that you shall live till youth is past.

'Tis to be remarked in this instance of mortality, in the death of this young person, that he was taken away in the midst of a time of awakening among many young persons in the town. And thereby, to show you what need you have to improve such times to your utmost, God shows you in this instance how uncertain you are that you shall live through this time of awakening it may be. This particular person doubtless hoped to have the benefit of it; he was endeavoring to make improvement of such an opportunity. He was much concerned for the salvation of his soul before he was taken sick; he was afraid of death and hell before there were any signs of the approaches of death; he was concerned how to get ready for death and eternity, and doubtless would have been much more distressed if he had known that there was but a step between him and eternity. There are probably but very few of you here present who are more awakened and more deeply concerned for the salvation of your souls than he was.

How loud, therefore, is the call of God to you in this providence to make haste and escape for your life, to improve the present day without putting anything off till tomorrow. Make haste and escape for your life; make haste and fly for refuge, and with all possible speed get into Christ so that you may be ready for death, however soon it may come. What a call is here to you to do your utmost to improve the present season of the pouring out of the Spirit of God while you have it, seeing that you do not know whether you shall live through it. What a call is here to you who are awakened and concerned as he was who is gone, to improve the time of the striving of God's Spirit to do your utmost so that soon your convictions may issue in conversion.

God has shown you what a great need you have of making haste, for death does not tarry for men. When the appointed time for men to die comes, they must die. They must not exceed the bounds that God has set by one inch, let their circumstances be what they will. If you are senseless and secure when the appointed time comes for you to die, you must go. Oh, therefore, let those who have hitherto neglected their souls neglect no longer.

Death won't wait. If you are found under deep concern at the time of death, it won't wait. Therefore let those who are under concerns improve their time.

Take heed of backsliding. If death should come when you are backsliding, how will you repent that you did not improve your time? If death comes upon you and finds you unprepared through your neglecting to take care and make haste, it will be your own fault; it will be your own foolish undoing. God has not been wanting in giving you warnings; you have certainly been much warned in the preaching of the Word.

God has taken the matter it into His own hands immediately to give you warning. He has shown you that you don't know how soon you may die. He has shown you that there is no passing the bounds that He has set.

The young person who lately died did not only die suddenly, but he was, through the greater part of his sickness, very much deprived of the use of his reason, which may show the folly of promising yourselves opportunity to seek salvation upon a deathbed.

God is going on still in His providence to warn you. Besides those young persons who have already launched forth into the boundless gulf of eternity, there is another young person who lives upon the brink of eternity with tuberculosis. It seems as though the time is near at hand when he also must leap into that great and endless eternity.

Now, therefore, you who are yet alive, who are on this side of eternity, in the enjoyment of a day of grace, hearken and take warning; be exhorted this day to now improve your time. Make haste, every one of you, to get into Christ where alone you can be safe.

Every one of you, make haste and be violent for the kingdom of heaven, as you have lately been directed. There is a necessity of it. What madness will it be for you to neglect it when you hear so much and see so much as you do? What a pity it is that you have lost as much time as you have. In all probability, most of you neglect your souls. Therefore lose no more time.

I can but exhort and beseech you; 'tis not in my power to save you; that is reserved for God alone. I can but set your necessity plainly before you. There are and will be some who will not regard what I have said. However, no one who has any due sense or due consideration of things can do any other than pity you, considering that you have now dying souls in you that must in a little time be either in heaven or hell.

Sensible persons who have any love to their fellow creatures can do no less than reason the case with you. How miserable you are while unprepared for death. You don't know how soon you must die; you don't know whether you shall have time to repent.

How happy you will be if you have an interest in Christ. You might be happy in this world; when you meet together, you might converse together of the things of God. This would be entertaining to you, and you would always be safe. And if you should die in youth, you would be happy.

3. These words are especially applicable to some of

those who may die in youth, some such as are peculiarly pleasant and are endowed with those pleasing qualifications. It was observed before that a flower is the most beautiful, pleasant, and fragrant part of the plant. It is most commonly put forth in the spring, the most pleasant part of the year, as was observed before, and then appears fair. It is also the most promising part of the plant, as it promises fruit. It may be observed of many flowers that the time of their opening themselves is in the morning; in the afternoon they close up.

This therefore is a fit emblem of a young person in the bloom of life, with amiable, pleasant, and promising qualifications; not only with a blooming body, but a blooming mind; a young person with desirable natural and moral endowments, giving hope of being comfortable, pleasant, and agreeable now to those who are round about, and of much fruit hereafter to be brought forth, of much future serviceableness in the world.

Such as these are sometimes cut down by death in their youth as a pleasant flower in the spring and morning is cut down by the scythe of the mower. Sometimes this is done suddenly, not by fading, as a leaf in the fall of the year, but as a flower that is cut down by the scythe: it is done at one stroke.

Application

Use of exhortation in two branches to prepare for death, first, to all to prepare for death, both young and old, and, second, particularly to young people.

1. To all, both young and old. The words of the text are spoken of mankind in general, though they are more especially applicable to young people. The Word of God shows the exceeding frailty of mankind in general at all ages, so God's providence, in the dispensa-

tions of it among us in the week past, first in the death of a young person in the bloom of youth, and then afterwards in the death of one advanced in years. As the providence of God in these things is calling on both old and young to be ready, so I would now take occasion to exhort all to get ready for death. Seeing your life is like a flower that is liable suddenly to be cut down and wither, therefore make haste to get that work done that must be done before death.

2. The second branch of the use is to exhort and beseech the young people of this congregation to prepare for death. You have lately had the truth of the words of the text set before you in a lively instance of one who lately died in this place in the very flower of youth. She was, the Sabbath before last here at the meeting. As of late she had been without any sensible signs of approaching death. But she too was suddenly cut down; she has now faded like a flower. Her place here in the house of God you can now see is empty.

This is a remarkable instance of human frailty and of the great uncertainty of life. In this case, after she was first taken ill, means were speedily used and physicians were constant from day to day while she lived; the advice of several physicians on her case was taken and the means used that they jointly agreed upon, but all was in vain; nothing prevailed. Notwithstanding all means that could be used, she soon departed. God's appointed time had come, and no means, care, or attendance by friends or physicians could avail to prevent death from doing its work.

This may be a warning to you not to trust or flatter yourself on anything for the preservation of your lives. Do not flatter yourself because at present you see no signs, or that now you are well enough to come into the house of God. Do not flatter yourself with any dependence or any care or means after you may be taken sick.

God has set your bounds; you do not know how near you are to death; when God's appointed time comes, nothing will serve you. This instance may warn you not to flatter yourself with hopes of much time to prepare after you are taken ill, or that you shall have any convenient season. It is usually far otherwise, as it was in this instance. Her pains and bodily distress from day to day were so great that if she had not taken care beforehand, she would have had but a poor opportunity.

Therefore let this instance be a warning to all you who are now here present, you who are now in your youth, without any delay to prepare for death. Is there not a great number of you young men and young women who now sit in this house who have no reason to think that you are prepared, no reason in the world to entertain a thought of your having any manner of preparation for death, because you are still a child of wrath?

It is astonishing how you can enjoy any comfort. How you can be so at ease? What would you do if you should in like manner be powerfully seized? How dismal would your case be, and what reason in the world is there for you to think that you shall not soon be seized? And what reason in the world have you of why you should delay?

What can you do in a Christless, graceless condition in that war? What will you do with that terrible enemy when he attacks? What will you do when your extremities grow cold and death begins to get hold of you? What will you do with death? Where will you look for comfort? What will you do for your poor soul that is going to leave the body?

How will you go into the eternal world? How will you appear before God? How will you make that leap?

And as to many of you who heretofore have had such extraordinary religious affections and thought you were converted, how it is now, after there has been a great deal of opportunity to see the nature, tendency, causes, and ways of the operation of your supposed grace and its consequences and fruits; when you consider these, is there any manner of reason to think that you are truly prepared for death? Have you any solid reason to think that your change was indeed that great change that the Scriptures speak of?

Will your building stand when the winds blow? Is there not great need that you should seek some better preparation for death, some better foundation of peace and comfort? You know in what way Christ tells you to seek salvation: you must strive to enter the kingdom with violence; you must make it your great business. So why will you delay to do so? Consider, is it wise? Is it reasonable? Let your own reason speak. Is it not worse than brutish folly to do otherwise?

But I would take occasion from this instance of that blooming flower that has lately been cut down by death to more particularly exhort the young people here present to the following things:

1. Avoid a light and vain conversation; don't let any filthy communication or conversation come out of your mouth. Don't delight in impure language contrary to that rule found in Colossians 3:8: "But now you also, put off all these: anger, wrath, malice, blasphemy, filthy communication." Don't delight in lascivious talking and jesting, in lewd and filthy songs contrary to the rule given in Ephesians 5:3-4: "But fornication, and all uncleanness, or covetousness, let it not be once named among you, as becometh saints; neither filthiness, nor foolish talking, nor jesting . . . ."

Avoid all profane speeches, speaking in a light manner of things that are of a sacred nature, as though you did not have much reverence towards God and things that are divine and religious. Avoid lightly bringing in these things to set off a joke and to enliven your diversions with them. It becomes Christians to observe that rule in Colossians 4:6: "Let your speech be always with grace, seasoned with salt."

When you meet together, contrive your conversation to often turn upon something that is in some respect profitable, tending to some instruction. Let it not be all vain, light, filthy, and empty, tending to nothing in the world but to amuse you, to waste away precious time, to establish more and more of a habit of levity and vanity, and to set you further and further in your disposition from anything that is serious, that tends to indispose you for all serious thoughts and concerns, and that will make you unfit for any religious and serious business. This will consequently make you unfit for death.

Such an empty, vain way of spending time is not becoming such poor, frail, dying creatures as men are. It administers no comfort to them on a deathbed; it will not be agreeable to reflect upon then.

There may be some diversions used by young people with moderation; this may be even in that which is both entertaining and profitable. But there is no need of levity, there is no need of meeting together for no reason but excite laughter.

Consider these three texts:

Ecclesiastes 2:2: "Laughter it is mad." Consider how unprofitable it is.

Proverbs 14:13: "The end of that mirth is heaviness."

Matthew 12:36: "For every idle word that men shall speak shall be brought into judgment."

Concerning her who has lately departed this life, some of you who had some acquaintance with her knew that she was of a contrary disposition to what has been said. She hated a vain conversation; she manifested in her living and dying a great delight in the society of the saints.

I would ask such now what they think, whether they suppose if it had been otherwise it could reasonably be so comfortable to us, her parents.

Could we have reviled the thoughts of such conversation and the ideas of what we saw when we saw bawdy behavior with so much comfort?

2. Avoid those liberties, that talk, and those customs used by young people in company; they are found by sufficient experience to lead to sin and to be of an evil and corrupt tendency. 'Tis the duty of Christians not only to avoid these things that are in themselves sinful, but also to avoid the very appearance of evil. For instance, we are to avoid not only the gross acts of lasciviousness, but such liberties as naturally tend to stir up lust.

That shameful, lascivious custom of handling women's breasts in public, and of different sexes lying in beds together. However light you may make of these, and may perhaps be involved in the custom of "frolicking," as it is called, your meeting together of companies of both sexes for drinking and the so general custom of being absent from family prayer and being out very late; those of different sexes sitting up late a great part of the night together—however light you may make of those things, and though perhaps you may be ready to make the reproving of those things only a mere matter of laughter and ridicule, yet I hope by the help of God I shall ever bear testimony against them as things of an evil and corrupt tendency. Such things have been the occasions of much sin; these things don't serve Christ's interests but the devil's. They are things that have been the devil's snares to thousands. They are things that don't prepare persons for death, but the contrary.

I do not doubt in the least but if any wise and considerate person will take the pains of an impartial reflection, consideration, and view of things, he must and will determine that such things are of pernicious consequences, and that they give Satan a great advantage. They would also see that it would greatly hurt the devil's interest if those things were banished from all Christian countries, and that thus the devil would be very sorry.

And I have no doubt but that those who have used those customs, if they impartially inquire of their own consciences, would admit that they never had any good come from them, but rather, on the contrary, that they actually tend to excite carnal affections, to hinder seriousness, that they tend to levity of mind, and indispose to serious meditation.

If this is so, they are unlawful. If they are dear as a right hand, yet they must be parted with. Matthew 5:29–30: "If thy right hand offend thee, cut it off."

If it is apparent that the devil has great advantage by them, then how is the practice of them consistent with that petition in the Lord's Prayer?

Let those who plead for these practices put it to themselves whether or not they don't believe in their hearts that the more serious persons are, the more engaged in religion they are, and the more naturally disposed they are to avoid those things that are light, vain, lustful, and senseless. He will be more inclined to be devout, to be constantly engaged in religion. He will be ever kept in solemn meditation; secret prayer is more likely to be upheld. But as for those who are much addicted to these things, inquire whether or not acts of fornication and unclean imaginations, whether frequent lustful desires aren't more commonly to be found in such as indulge themselves than in others who strictly avoid them; whether gross acts of uncleanness aren't much more frequently committed.

Are these things consistent with a pouring out of

the Spirit of God? If we go through the world, aren't these things found most among those who have least religion, and the least seriousness and preparation for death?

Now if this is so, how can these things be accounted for? If so, then how does it come to pass that you are so involved in matters that only concern your temporal interest? Would we have God in His providence deal so with us?

We are often commanded to avoid those things that tend to lead others into sin. 1 Corinthians 8:8–13: "But meat commendeth us not to God: for neither, if we eat, are we the better; neither, if we eat not, are we the worse. But take heed lest by any means this liberty of yours become a stumblingblock to them that are weak. For if any man see thee which hast knowledge sit at meat in the idol's temple, shall not the conscience of him which is weak be emboldened to eat those things which are offered to idols; and through thy knowledge shall the weak brother perish, for whom Christ died? But when ye sin so against the brethren, and wound their weak conscience, ye sin against Christ. Wherefore, if meat make my brother to offend, I will eat no flesh while the world standeth, lest I make my brother to offend."

Romans 14:13: "Let us not therefore judge one another any more: but judge this rather, that no man put a stumblingblock or an occasion to fall in his brother's way."

Romans 14:15: "But if thy brother be grieved with thy meat, now walkest thou not charitably. Destroy not him with thy meat, for whom Christ died."

Romans 14:20–21: "For meat destroy not the work of God. All things indeed are pure; but it is evil for that man who eateth with offense. It is good neither to eat flesh, nor to drink wine, nor any thing whereby thy brother stumbleth, or is offended, or is made weak."

If we must not lead others into sin, surely we must not lead ourselves into it!

Another thing I would desire you to consider seriously with yourself is whether your having practiced these things will afford any comfort on a deathbed, or whether or not it would be more comfortable if you should die in the bloom of youth, as one has lately done among us.

One thing more I would put to you, whether, if you should die in the flower of youth, you can think it could reasonably be any matter of comfort to your parents for them to say, "My departed child was an eminent frolicker, much of a gallant, a jolly companion."

In this matter you may easily believe that I am speaking sensibly. The person aforementioned who lately died in the bloom of her youth was one of my own dear children. I now know how comfortable it is in such a case for a parent to consider regarding his departed child to have the greatest evidence that his child strictly avoided those customs, practices, and liberties that I have mentioned, that have been so customary among young people. My dear child never manifested any inclination to any of these things, but had them constantly in abhorrence, as I doubt not but some of you who had some acquaintance with her are fully sensible. I can now be sensible of what a bitterness it would be to me if it had been contrarywise.

And as the young person that I am now speaking of was a young woman, so I would on this occasion particularly address myself to the young women here present. Let me now on this occasion, which is to me, as you will easily believe, very heavy and sorrowful, earnestly advise and exhort you not to practice nor allow for such liberties as have been spoken of. But, on the contrary, keep to rules of stricter virtue in your conversation, which will be far more for your comfort, far more for your peace of conscience, more for your honor, credit, and esteem, and in every way more for your advantage, as to this world and that which is to come.

Such liberties as have been spoken are especially foolish and dishonorable in your sex, being so contrary to that strict modesty which is in the eyes of mankind so much to the glory of your sex. And it is a rule that will evermore hold good that the more free those of your sex are in such liberties and the more easily they are prevailed upon to yield to them, the more despicable creatures they become even in the eyes of them who at present seem pleased, and will flatter them and pretend to laugh at them.

To gain their purpose and gratify their own evil inclinations, and because the contrary crosses their inclination, they will laugh at you till they see you are unconquerable. Their desire is that nothing be good, but rather that it become more cheap, mean, servile, and contemptible in this world.

Besides this there is the wound you give your souls, and the guilt and ruin you bring upon them. Therefore, such things become a foundation of dark sorrow, gloominess, and dismal darkness on a deathbed.

It will in every way be better for you to be strict, to walk in the ways of the strictest virtue, decency, and honor, and with immovable resolution and steadiness maintain your ground. This will be most for your honor and esteem, most for your comfort, most for the peace and quiet of your conscience when you come to die, and will tend most to the eternal salvation of your souls.

3. Another thing that I would now take occasion of from the late instance of death in one in the young persons is to exhort you to dutifulness to your parents.

'Tis what many young people greatly fail in, in not hearkening to their counsels. They are not careful to please their parents. This is exceedingly contrary to the disposition of that person I am speaking of; she was a remarkeable instance of honor, respect, and duty to parents. She not only maintained a most strict and conscientious regard to their advice and counsel, but she was disposed to ask their counsel in all important affairs. She sought studiously and with great care and concern to please them and to avoid anything that might be grievous to them. She seemed ever deeply concerned for their comfort and exerted herself to the utmost to that end.

4. Don't set your heart on youthful pleasures and other vain enjoyments of this world, nor employ yourself mainly in pursuit of them. If you would be ready for death, your heart must be taken off from such things and must be brought to place your happiness in virtue and piety.

How dreadful must death be to such young people as set their affections on the things of this world; and, on the contrary, how much will it be for your comfort to be ready for death when it comes.

It may be thought to be from the fondness and tender affections of a parent towards a deceased child that I here mention again the example of my daughter Jerusha, but so far as I know my own heart, what I shall say of her at this time is not so much to seek her honor and my own as it is for your profit. She has long appeared to be a person who was remarkably weaned from the things of this world.

Some of you have shown affection on the occasion of her death, talking about her heart and her being very indifferent about all things whatsoever of a worldly nature; how her heart was steadily governed by a great desire, and how she manifested a relish and appetite to choose God for her supreme good. She declared in words and showed in deeds that she was ever ready to deny herself. In every affair she earnestly inquired in which way she could most glorify God, do the most service, and be under the best advantages for her soul's good.

These things appeared in her not as a slight affection, but they seemed to be the steady, habitual, reigning disposition and bent of her mind, governing her in her whole conduct. And she declared on her deathbed that she could say without any doubt or hesitation that she had not seen any other good in the world besides an opportunity to serve and glorify God in it; and she added that she never could see anything else in the world worth living for. She declared that it had ever been so with her that the more clear views she had of God, the more comfort and hope she had; she appeared vastly the more mean and more sinful in her own eyes, and also ever found the most strong and lively hungerings and thirstings after grace and holiness.

5. Therefore on this occasion I would lastly exhort you to examine and search yourselves, you who have entertained a hope of heaven, of what sort your religion has been. Has it consisted only or chiefly in transient flights and pangs, in a morning cloud, or has it consisted in a habitual relish, choice, bent, and determination of mind for God and holiness as the supreme good. The Word of God is our rule, and this is certainly not a morning cloud, not like the light of a comet (Jude 13).

And what have been the fruits and consequences of your supposed discoveries, joys, and great affections? Have they caused you to make religion your business? Have the service of God, His glory, and your own increase in holiness become the steady pursuits of your life, what you have in practice chiefly sought after, accounting worldly things despicable by comparison?

Let me entreat you to consider what you have been doing, how you have spent your time since this young person died. God, in the late instance of the death of a young person, is showing you what need you have to be determined concerning your hope, as it shows you how liable you are suddenly and with but little warning to be snatched out of the world.

It is has been a sad and doleful time among us for several years with regard to the state of religion among both young and old. God's calls and warnings in His Word have been very many; especially has God been remarkeably testifying to this for the last three years. Many young people have died, but yet we have continued in sin. Oh, that this instance of death might be a means of reviving and awakening the young people! I pray that this will be a means of solemnizing them and leading them to serious consideration, giving a new turn to their thoughts, concerns, and conversations, reviving religion among them, and being the beginning of a general awakening and reformation among you, the young people of my flock. It would abundantly add comfort to the circumstances of this providence, which itself is so bitter and afflictive to me.

I should think I had much more cause to admire God's mercy in such a happy consequence than to mourn for our own loss, though it is so great, and though the enjoyment God has taken away, as you are doubtless sensible, at least many of you were so pleasant and comfortable while God continued it.

10

Don't Lead Others into Sin

"Wherefore if meat make my brother to offend, I will eat no flesh while the world standeth lest I make my brother to offend." 1 Corinthians 8:13

The immediate occasion of the apostle's writing this epistle to the Corinthians seems to have been their writing to him for his advice and direction concerning several important articles. This appears by the first verse of the seventh chapter: "Now concerning the things which ye wrote to me." One of these things that they wrote to the apostle about was touching things offered to idols, whether or not when they were invited by their heathen friends and neighbors to a feast on their heathen festival days, where things offered to idols were eaten, whether or not they might not go. Some of them scrupled it and others among them it seems did not scruple it, but supposed that it was as lawful to eat that meat as any other meat, and that its having been offered to an idol in no way changed the nature or quality of the meat. They accounted it to be only from weakness and ignorance that anyone made any scruple of it.

It is to those latter ones that the apostle principally directs himself, and he doesn't enter into any dispute with them whether or not those who scrupled to eat things offered to idols were not weak and ignorant, and whether they who were not troubled with any such scruples were not the more knowing. He only warns them not to be too conceited of their knowledge, and warns them not to hurt and wound the souls of those whom they accounted their weak brethren by their practice of eating things offered to idols. Verse 9: "But take heed lest this liberty of yours become a stumbling block to them that are weak," that is, this liberty that you take to eat things offered to idols.

Then the apostle goes on in verses 10–12: "For if anyone sees you who have knowledge eating in an idol's temple, will not the conscience of him who is weak be embolded to eat those things offered to idols? And because of your knowledge, shall the weak brother perish, for whom Christ died? But when you thus sin against the brethren, and wound their weak conscience, you sin against Christ."

The case was this: There were many of the Corinthian Christians who were already under great temptation to eat things offered to idols living among the heathen, and were often invited by their heathen relations to come to those feasts. And it was against the consciences of many of the good Christians of Corinth to comply with this practice, though they were under so great a temptation to. And if some Christians went who would greatly increase the temptation to others, for then, besides the invitations of their heathen friends, they would have the examples of their Christian brethren to influence and tempt them, and would be in great danger of being influenced by their example to comply when indeed their consciences were not satisfied about it. And thus their taking such a liberty would prove a stumbling block and snare to others. This is the reason of the words of the apostle in the text: "Wherefore, if meat make my brother stumble, I will never again eat meat lest I make my brother stumble."

I would observe two things in the words:

1. The evil to be avoided that the apostle here speaks of, which is making his brother to offend or leading

his brother into sin.

2. The means he would be willing to use to avoid this evil: he would eat no meat while the world stood, which would be a great instance of self-denial. But we are to understand that the apostle would look upon it as his duty to deny himself his own pleasure or the gratification of his outward appetite to any degree rather than lead his brother into sin to the wounding of his soul. He should regard the spiritual welfare of his brother before any gratification of his senses or natural appetites. As he says in Romans 14:21: "It is good neither to eat flesh nor to drink wine, nor anything whereby thy brother stumbleth or is offended or is made weak."

And the apostle, to confirm what he says, goes on in the chapter 9 to tell of as great and greater instances of self-denial than this, that he had actually complied with for the sake of others' souls, such as his not taking wages for his labor as he had power to do, but working with his own hands; his restraining from marrying for the sake of the furtherance of the gospel; his becoming as a Jew to the Jews that he might gain the Jews.

DOCTRINE: We ought to be exceedingly careful that we don't lead others into sin. We see that the Apostle Paul declared that, rather than do this, he stood ready rather to deny himself for his whole lifetime a common enjoyment and priviledge of mankind, and an enjoyment which Providence has indulged to him as well as the rest of mankind. It would be a daily self-denial, but he woud be willing to undergo this self-denial of his otherwise lawful appetite every day that he lived rather than cause a brother to stumble or lead another into sin by it.

Paul did not speak this because he looked upon himself as being under greater obligations to be strictly careful to avoid leading others into sin than other men; for he says what he says here on purpose that it might be for the direction of others that he wrote to.

In speaking to this doctrine, I will mention some of the ways wherein one man may lead others into sin, and then give reasons why we should be careful not to do so.

1. Persons oftentimes lead others into sin by persuading and enticing them. Oftentimes this is done when persons would make use of others either as instruments of their wickedness or as their assistants in it, and would strengthen their own hands by it; when they have a mind to have a number with them in the same guilt, hoping for the more indemnity. And by this means or that the blame or reproach that will be procured by it may not lie so heavy upon them. Or, when they would have others partner with them, that with them and by them they may gratify their lusts, as when some tempt others to be guilty of uncleanness with them either in a greater or lesser degree. In this case they entice others and endeavor to lead them into sin because they can't fulfill their lusts and accomplish their impure desires without some others being guilty with them.

But oftentimes wicked men, when they don't need to have others joining with them in sin upon any such account, yet they will endeavor to persuade and entice others to the same sins that they themselves are guilty of. 'Tis the nature of wickedness to desire to propagate itself, as it is the nature of holiness. Godly men desire to have others be godly; so it is the nature of vice and wickedness to. Sin loves to spread and propagate itself. This nature of sin appeared in the first being that sinned. Satan tempted man to sin. After the woman had sinned, she tempted the man.

Satan's kingdom has all along endeavored to uphold itself in the world. Those who are of that kingdom

have endeavored to promote it and oppose the kingdom of Christ. This is remarkable among heretics and
those of pernicious principles in religion: they are like
the Pharisees of old who compassed sea and land to
make one proselyte (Matthew 23:15).

2. Another way that men lead others into sin is by
their example. Example has a mighty influence upon
men, especially evil examples. Men are already, by the
violent corruptions and evil inclinations of their own
nature, so strongly prejudiced in favor of and disposed
to fall in with sin. Example takes off the restraints, it
takes off the dread that men have of wickedness. When
persons see others do it boldly, and see that it is a frequent, common practice, it makes it not to seem such a
dreadful thing. Yea, common example tends to make
things credible, or at least not disgraceful; for what is it
for anything to be disgraceful but commonly to be reputed odious and a cause of shame among men? But
anything naturally ceases to be commonly so reputed
when it comes to be a common practice; for men, by
their practice, show their minds. They show their approbation of anything. There is a language in practice,
and persons do as much thereby and more effectually
declare their minds to others in favor of what they practice more than if they endeavored to persuade men by
all the arguments they could use to commit the same.

The prevailing of wicked customs and practices of
all kinds in the world arises very much from ill example; the prevailing of any bad ways or practices in particular towns commonly and chiefly arises from example. One learns from another and is emboldened by
another. The prevailing of vicious practices among
young people is chiefly from example; one learns from
another. One may infect a multitude; one may infect a
whole town, and one generation of young people
learns from another, the following from the foregoing.

Indeed, one man, by the same example as another, may do ten times as much towards leading others into sin. A person's influence by example is in proportion to the esteem and reputation they have among others; their influence is in proportion to their authority and the like. Such therefore do a great deal more hurt by their ill example. And persons are likely to do much hurt with those whom they have most interest in, as parents to their children.

Persons by their example may be an occasion of others being led into sin whom they never conversed with; their evil ways may be propagated from one to another, like an infectious distemper, and may descend to successive generations.

3. Men lead others into sin by seeming to favor or countenance any wickedness, when persons either plead for wickedness, or stand up for them who have been guilty, pleading for the lawfulness of this or that corrupt practice, or extenuating it, endeavoring to make others think that it is not so heinous a thing. Even if persons do not directly plead for any practice, yet if they seem to countenance it, speak lightly of it, making a jest of it, speaking of it as if it were not a very dreadful thing, speaking of it without any such marks of abhorrence or disallowance as might justly be expected in a thing of such a nature, they may do a great deal towards leading others into sin by this means. This is especially true if they are leading men of reputation and influence. Such a man may do more hurt by only speaking in such a manner of any bad practice as to seem to make it a light matter than if he should plead for it with all his might. Men may do considerably towards forwarding any prevailing wickedness by their silence only, by not appearing against it to bear a testimony against it and put a stop to it.

So a man may be guilty of hardening another in sin

by his not reproving him for it. He may interpret his silence as an approbation of his wickedness, and that may be just occasion for putting such a construction upon it.

4. Men lead others to sin by laying before them the occasions of sin. Thus, by causing or contributing to any contention, occasion is given for a great deal of sins being committed; for where there is contention, there is confusion and every evil (James 3:16). So persons may be guilty of leading others into sin by leading them into such circumstances in any respect as that they shall have temptations to sin laying before them. Perhaps they do so by leading them into bad company or into intimacy with persons of a vicious character, or by laying before any person the fuel of his predominant lust. An example is when persons give strong drink to any man who is especially addicted to excessive drinking. Many other ways might be mentioned wherein persons may bring others into snares, lay stumbling blocks before them, and be an occasion of great wounds to their souls.

Here I will give some reasons why we ought to be exceeding careful not to lead others into sin.

1. Hereby we shall be an occasion of dishonor to the name of God. As we ought superlatively to love God, so the honor and glory of God ought to be very dear to us, and we ought not only to be careful that we don't dishonor God directly by what we do ourselves, but we ought as we are able to endeavor that He may be honored in the world. We ought to endeavor to promote His glory in the world and the advancement of His kingdom and interest, and ought to our utmost to endeavor to prevent His being dishonored among men. God has made us for His own glory, and He expects that His glory should be dear to us, and that we should endeavor to promote it by all opportunities, and to the

utmost of our power. But if instead of that we lead others to dishonor the holy name of God, we shall greatly provoke God and make ourselves most guilty in His sight.

We are guilty of dishonoring God enough by our own sins; we have no need to lead others to dishonor Him too. We have brought dishonor enough, and too much, to God's holy name with our own hands; we need not take others along with us to assist us. If sin is a great evil, and very hateful upon the account that it is a dishonor to God, then it is hateful in others upon the same account. We ought to hate it whenever we see it and not be the causes or occasions of it. We ought to look upon disobedience to God and dishonoring Him as infinite evils, wherever they are; and therefore nothing should be sufficient to tempt us to be the occasions of it or accessories to it.

Well might the apostle say that he would eat no meat while the world stood rather than be guilty of it. When we lead others into sin, we know not how much dishonor to God it will be an occasion of, how much sin in him that one may be the occasion of, how often repeated it may be, how it may lead him into a bad custom that he may never get rid of. That sin may be the occasion of many other sins, for one sin tends to bring on others. We know not how far it will be propagated, as when we give another an infectious distemper we know not but that it will be an occasion of thousands having it who would not have had it otherwise.

2. We may be an occasion of infinite mischief to the souls of others. If we lead others into sin, we give their souls a dreadful wound; we give them a mortal wound. Every sin that any man commits is in itself a mortal wound to his soul, a wound that in its own nature must prove mortal were it not for some remedy of infinite grace and power's providing. When we lead others into

sin, we do what lies within us to destroy and undo another forever; we do what in its own nature naturally tends to his eternal destruction, and would necessarily issue in it were it not for the infinite grace and power of God. And therefore the apostle, in dissuading the Christians that he wrote to from leading others into sin by their own liberties, makes use of this as an argument with them, that herein they will destroy him whom they lead into sin. Note the 11th verse: "and through thy knowledge shall the weak brother perish." And Romans 14:15: "Destroy not him with thy meat for whom Christ died." And verse 20: "for meat destroy not the work of God."

If we lead others into sin, it is no thanks to us if it doesn't issue in their eternal damnation; it is not owing to us, it is owing to the redeeming love and grace of God in Jesus Christ. If Christ had not died and shed His infinitely precious blood for sin, it must necessarily and unavoidably have issued in their eternal ruin, in their everlasting misery and torment. So dreadful a thing is the evil that we have been the occasion of to our neighbor that nothing but the very blood of the Son of God can save him from eternal destruction as the issue of it.

If we stab another man in the heart, it is no thanks to us if he isn't killed, though God shoud save his life by a miracle. But there is need of an infinitely greater thing to be done than the working of such a miracle in order to save a man from eternal destruction after we have led him into sin. It is a greater thing for the Son of God to take on Him men's nature and dwell here in flesh, and at last to spill His own blood, and then to heal the soul by the infinite power of His own Spirit, than merely to work a miracle to save a man's temporal life after he has received a mortal wound. But all this is necessary to save a man from eternal destruction after

we have been guilty of leading him into sin. And when
we have led a man into sin, we don't know but that will
be the issue of it, that is, his perishing to all eternity; we
don't know whether God will ever give him repentance;
we don't know but that that very sin will be the occasion of his ruin, will be the occasion of his being hardened in sin and led in to a wicked way so as to prevent
him from ever coming to God, or that it will provoke
God forever to leave him and give him up to sin. We
don't know if he would have perished if he had not
committed that sin. Yet his misery will be infinitely
greater because of that sin. There will be an eternal
punishment for that sin that will be in addition to his
misery more than would have been if he had not committed that sin, and that addition will remain to all
eternity. It will be an eternal addition to his misery and
torment, which will be an infinite evil. The least degree
of pain or addition of pain that is eternal is infinitely
worse and more dreadful than any temporal suffering
whatsoever because it is eternal.

So by leading others into sin we shall bring the
guilt of the blood of souls upon our hands. God may
require their blood at our hands, and what a heavy bur-
den will that be! What a dreadful thing to have the guilt
of the blood of souls upon us. When we have the guilt
of murdering our neighbor's soul and bringing him to
his eternal ruin and damnation, how can we answer
this, when God shall charge us with it? It would be a
great injury to our neighbor if we should burn his
house, destroy his estate, or kill him. But is it not a
greater injury to ruin and undo his soul to all eternity?

We do not know how great an undoing we may
bring, or how many souls we shall undo. By leading a
person into one sin, we may be the occasion of a thousand to one man, as we observed before. Persons who
lead others into sin are often an occasion of sin in

multitudes. As we observed, most of the prevailing of
sin and wickedness that there is in towns or in the
world is from bad examples, and from being led into
sin by others. The guilt, the blood of how many souls
then do those leaders bring upon themselves? Men may
be instruments of transmitting wickedness to posterity,
and so of undoing souls in future generations.

What need have we to bring the guilt of the blood of
souls upon us? Will it not be sufficient for us to damn
our own souls? But must we also be guilty of damning
many others?

3. Hereby we shall be partakers in other men's sin.
Is not our own guilt sufficient, and as much as we can
bear? Is not that punishment and torment enough, to
bear the guilt of those sins that may especially and
more peculiarly be called our own original sin, all our
actual transgressions? Must we go and make ourselves
partakers of the guilt of others' wickedness, of scores
and hundreds of others?

4. Hereby we do the devil's work and become the
devil's instruments. It is the devil's work to lead others
to sin; he was the first who ever did it; he began it in
this world, tempting Eve. It is his daily work in the
world. And shall we do his work? Then we shall be
Satan's tools. We shall hereby appear to be Satan's sol-
diers to carry on the designs of his kingdom and to oppose the kingdom of Jesus Christ.

Application

USE OF INSTRUCTION. We ought to do our utmost
to lead others to righteousness. If leading others into
sin is a thing so exceedingly to be avoided, then it will
follow that leading others to the contrary of sin is exceedingly to be sought and endeavored. If leading oth-

ers into sin is to be avoided because it is to the dishonor of God, then promoting virtue, religion, and
piety in others ought to be sought and endeavored because it tends to the glory of God. If leading
others into sin is to be avoided with exceeding care because it tends to the eternal ruin and mischief of others' souls, which is infinitely greater mischief than any
temporal calamity we can bring upon anyone, then we
ought earnestly to endeavor to lead them to righteousness, because hereby we shall be in the way to have the
reward of the good we have done. Hereby we shall be a
means of promoting Christ's kingdom and interest.

We ought to be exceedingly careful to avoid leading
others into sin because thereby we do the devil's work
and become Satan's instruments. And if we do Christ's
works, we shall be co-workers with Him, for this is the
work of Christ, a work that He glories in. One of the
most glorious works that He is the Author of is to make
us His instruments. Providence puts into all persons'
hands opportunities and advantages more or less for
doing good in this respect, for promoting Christ's
kingdom in the world, and for promoting the interest
of virtue. There are scarcely any, and perhaps none at
all, but what have some degree of influence upon others, and they may improve their influence this way.

There are some special favorable opportunities to
promote religion that Providence gives men if they
would watch and observe them, and have but a thorough disposition to improve them. Indeed, this is an affair in which there is need of our excercising our best
wisdom and prudence. We ought to make it our study to
find opportunities and to obtain advantages for the
successful endeavoring of promoting virtue and religion. Persons don't excuse themselves from other affairs and business upon which their own temporal interest depends because some difficulty attends it. And

there is need of care and skill in order to successfully manage these. But they are content to make it their study and to use their best contrivances and diligence. And so surely we ought in this affair wherein we serve God and Christ, and do the work that we are called to as Christ's disciples and subjects. If everyone did but make it as much his study and contrivance by all means and opportunities to promote religion in the world as they do in the management of their own secular affairs, what a mighty tendency would it have to make religion gloriously to flourish and to be a means of the conversion and salvation of multitudes of souls!

Some men have great advantages in their hands, having greater influence than their neighbors. How may it well be expected by their Maker that they especially should endeavor to promote religion and lead others to righteousness. 'Tis God who has given them their influence and put them under such advantages, and committed the same to them as a talent to be improved for this purpose. "Those to whom much is given, of them much is required" (Luke 12:48).

We ought to use our utmost endeavors to reclaim vicious persons by discountenancing their vices and bearing a testimony against them, to them, or before them, and doing this by reproving them or otherwise showing a dislike and abhorrence of their ways. If vicious persons saw that their vices were generally abhorred and detested by others, and they got nothing but general dislike and disgrace upon the account, there would not be so many going on in their vices as now do; yea, if they only saw that leading men, and those who were in credit and esteem for natural abilities, wealth, or otherwise. Vice prevails and rides triumphant because it is no great matter of shame to be vicious, and vicious persons find enough who like them little or nothing the worse, and therefore they are not ashamed of their vices. So wicked practices prevail and spread for that which is a principal restraint to wickedness is removed.

We ought to use our utmost endeavors to bring others to conviction. When we see others being stupid, senseless, and negligent of their souls, we ought, as we have advantage and opportunity, to labor to make them sensible of the danger of the state they are in, of the great importance of eternity, of the shortness and uncertainty of life, and to bring them to think much of dying and going to appear before God. We ought to endeavor to make them sensible of the dreadfulness of enduring the torments of hell to all eternity. When we see others whom we are concerned about, who are under our care or influence, and who seem to be senseless and negligent of their souls, we ought not to be easy till we see them be more sensible and careful.

We ought to do our utmost to promote the going on of the work of conversion in the place where we live. Indeed, by endeavoring to procure the conviction and awakening of others we shall do this. To this end, the ministers of the gospel ought always to be assisted and strengthened.

We ought to promote others' holiness of life. The apostle is often exhorting Christians to be doing those things which shall be for mutual edification. 1 Thessalonians 5:11: "Edify one another as also ye do." 1 Corinthians 14:26: "Let all things be done to edifying." We ought to do this by our example. Our lights should so shine before men that they will see our good works and glorify our Father who is in heaven (Matthew 5:16). We can also do this by living a holy life. A bright example in saints tends exceedingly to commend religion to others, and particularly to stir up other saints to live more holily; for therein they have the beauty of a holy life set before their eyes. They don't only hear it described in words, but they actually see it in an instance, which has a vastly greater tendency to give us a lively idea of it than by the hearing of it.

This ought to be done also by mutual communication and conversing together of the things of God and religion. Such things ought frequently to be the subjects of the communication of Christians when they are together, so that they may stir up and quicken one another, admonishing and comforting one another. Ephesians 4:29: "Let no corrupt conversation proceed out of your mouth, but that which is good to the use of edification, that it may minister grace to the hearer."

That which persons talk about, that they will be apt to think about. Conversation tends mightily to engage the thoughts and turn them that way about these things that our conversation is upon.

We ought as much as in us lies to endeavor to promote Christian knowledge in the places where we live and among those with whom we are concerned. Knowledge is the key that opens to all else that pertains to religion. It is called the key of knowledge in Luke 11:52. This may be promoted by us among our neighbors by taking opportunities to fall into and promote talk about any principle or points of religion, endeavoring to inform ourselves and one another in our talk upon such subjects. And we especially ought to promote knowledge by taking pains to instruct those who are under our care and instruction; we ought to diligently lead their minds in a good and distinct understanding of the principles of religion by laying things open to them in a manner adapted to their capacity. We should countenance and forward any public means used for the upholding and promoting of knowledge.

These things especially ought to be done by those who are of the same family, one to another. Those who are in that near relationship of husbands and wives are under very great advantages to promote virtue and religion one to the other. And so those who are brothers and sisters, who dwell together under the same roof, or even if they are scattered, yet their near relationship and intimate acquaintance gives them great advantage.

But above all, parents ought to do this toward their children. 'Tis especially their duty which God expects, and most strictly requires of them, to labor diligently to instruct and to restrain them from all vicious practices by precept and government, to warn them and labor to deeply impress their minds with a sense of the great things of another world. Make your children sensible of the danger of sin, of death, of judgment, and of hell. Be often stirring them up, leading them into virtuous and religious practices, setting for them a good example.

All Christians should strive in this matter by their prayers to promote religion in families, among friends, among acquaintances, in towns, in other lands, and in the world.

USE OF EXAMINATION. Let this doctrine put all upon examining themselves, whether or not they have not been guilty of leading others into sin. Have you not been guilty of enticing others to sin? Have you at one time and another done the devil's work in tempting others, and endeavoring to persuade them to comply with you in wicked designs and practices? Haven't you led many others to be your companions in wickedness? And have you not reason to think that you have promoted sin and ill customs and practices among others by countenancing them, by pleading for the practices themselves, or for those who have been guilty of them? Have you not been guilty of pleading for Baal? Have you not spoken of these and those vices with an air that has manifested your making light of them, as if you did not account them as very dreadful things?

Haven't you reason to think that others have been emboldened in wickedness by what you have said, or by your silence, holding your peace when you ought to have spoken and borne a testimony? Haven't you reason to think that by your wickedness many others have been led on to be wicked, and that wickedness has prevailed the more because of you? Haven't you reason to think that many more have addicted themselves to such and such a vice because of you? Haven't you been a leader in wickedness? Haven't you reason to think that there has been less virtue and a greater prevailing of vice and unwarrantable practices than if you had never been born, and that there is now, even at this day, more wickedness in the town than if you never had been born, or had died when you were an infant? Would it not have been well for many poor souls, and well for the interest of religion, if you never had been born?

Think seriously on this matter and judge impartially concerning yourself whether it is so or not. Consider it, and let your consciences speak without a bribe. Are there not some who are now going on in such ways that have a tendency to lead others to sin, to corrupt and debauch their mind, vitiate their principles, and pervert their ways? 1 Corinthians 15:33: "Evil communications corrupt good manners."

I would desire heads of families particularly to put it to themselves, whether they haven't reason to think that they have been the occasion of leading their children to sin, that they have depraved and vitiated the minds of children. Such is the mutual relationship and circumstances of parents and children that children naturally learn from their parents and are influenced by them, especially when they are little. As an infant sucks its mother's breasts, the child is, as it were, naturally molded and fashioned by beholding its parents, by

what it sees them do from time to time and hears them
say, by seeing what they like and what they dislike. By
being constantly under the influence of their judgment, inclinations, and ways, the child grows up from a
state of nonentity under these things, and under the
influence of them conforms naturally to them like wax
to the seal, as it were; they naturally grow into such a
shape and are cast into that mold.

If there is anything in the parent that tends to influence the child, either good or bad, the child is more
easily influenced, being tender and yieldable. Like soft
wax, you may make what impression you will upon it, or
as a young twig that is easily turned and set, growing
this way or that way.

When they are young, they are newly come into the
world and their minds, as to any prepossessions or
prejudices of any judgment already formed or habit
contracted, are like white paper: you may write or lay
what colors you will upon it—though when once it is
colored or written on, it is not so easily altered afterwards.

Let everyone who has children, or others whom they
have brought up, examine how it is in their families.
What impressions have been made upon your children
by your influence, by what they have seen in you or
heard from you? Haven't you set such an example? Hasn't your way of communicating been such in
their sight, your way of ordering and regulating yourself and your family been such that your children's
minds have naturally been depraved? And is there not a
prospect of their proving to be irreligious and persons
of ill morals very much by this means?

There is a great difference in some families, though
it is to be lamented so few. The children are sober, well-
behaved, accustomed to good order, decent in their
carriage, respectful to superiors, and the like. Others

are more like the children of heathens: without any religion or manners, rude and disorderly. To what is such a difference ordinarily to be attributed but to the difference there is in the parents' walking before them and their manner of educating their children? Haven't you reason to fear that you have been in a great measure the murderers of your own children's souls? Haven't you led them into sin, confirmed them in sin, and hardened their hearts in sin, instead of restraining them from sin, leading them into ways of religion and virtue, warning, admonishing, instructing, and training them up in the nurture and admonition of the Lord, as you ought to have done?

It may be that your children are yet unconverted and unawakened. Might it not probably have been otherwise, at least some of them, if you had done your duty towards them?

It may be that some of your children are dead, and they died without giving any probable signs of conversion. And you have reason to be afraid whether or not they have gone to hell. And if it is so, haven't you reason to accuse yourself for having had a great hand in it? Or, if your children should die in a Christless state and condition, and so be damned to all eternity, would there not be reason for you to condemn yourself in that you and the devil joined together to forward your children's damnation?

I will conclude with a few words for the awakening and warning of those who are guilty of leading others into sin.

Consider how awful and dreadful a thing it is to carry the blood and the guilt of souls around with you. If you have been a means of others' damnation by your leading them into sin, you have the guilt of their blood lying at your door.

Persons are chargeable with the consequences of

their sins, if they have been warned of those consequences. If persons, by doing that which God has forbidden them, are the occasion of mischief following
on themselves or others, God justly charges them with
it, if they were warned of those consequences, were
forewarned of the tendency of their sins to those consequences, or the danger there was of those things following.

Thus if a person, when he has been forewarned, is
the occasion of the ruin and everlasting perdition of
another's soul, he is chargeable before God of that
mischief, that is, that soul's everlasting perdition. If his
sin has been the occasion of the damnation of a hun-
dred others by spreading an infection descending to
later generations, the loss and eternal misery of all
those souls is chargeable upon him, for he was forewarned of the danger of those consequences, and yet
committed it anyway.

And though he certainly did not know that they
would follow, yet he knew that they might follow, and
that then their sin inferred some danger of it.

If you lead others on to sin, yet know not what the
consequences will be, you know not to what a dismal
and dreadful degree, how great the misery of how many
will be; but this you do know, that they must be very ill.
And as we said before, you are guilty of the damnation
of souls, as much as in you lies. You have stabbed them
to the heart, and that wound will be mortal unless infinite power and grace prevents, which will be no thanks
to you.

It is a dreadful thing to have the guilt of a person's
blood, of destroying temporal lives. All nations have
this apprehension, that it is a dreadful thing to have
the guilt of murder. The heathen of old held to this, as
may be seen by what the inhabitants of the Isle of Malta
said of Paul. When Paul had been bitten by a viper, they

said, "No doubt this man is a murderer" (Acts 28:4). They had the notion that a murderer ordinarily could not escape vengeance.

How dreadful then to have the guilt of the blood of souls! Abel's blood cried out for vengeance. But how do the poor lost souls cry for vengeance from hell! Temporal death is a great calamity, to be guilty of blood. Consider how much greater eternal damnation is. Let parents consider, you would be angry with anyone for striking or abusing your children; how dreadful is it to be guilty of the souls of children.

If you have been a leader of others into sin, how do you know but that there are now souls in hell whose damnation you have been an occasion of? 'Tis most probable that it is so, if you have been one who has had a great hand in bringing in or promoting the corruption of manners. And it is also probable that many more will be damned by your means. If there are some now in hell whose damnation you have been the occasion of, how do they curse you for your cruelty to them! They curse the day that ever they were acquainted with you, that ever you were born, as it only augmented their misery.

And you who have led your children into sin, and have taken no care of their souls, but have corrupted them by your example, consider those whom you have led into sin, you are in danger of having them rise up in judgment against you at the day of judgment, if God doesn't convert many and wash away your guilt in the blood of His Son. If you are thereby the occasion of the damnation of the souls of others, you will then have them rising up in judgment against you, accusing you, crying out against you before the Judge: "This man has been the occasion of my ruin. He corrupted and vitiated my mind. He tempted me to sin; he led me into such a vicious course; he hardened my heart in wickedness; he laid snares in my way. It is he who has been one great occasion of my eternal ruin!"

Many a damned child will then rise up in judgment against his parents and say, "This, my father, or this, my mother, was a great occasion of my ruin. He or she took no care of my soul. They were not concerned for my salvation; they did not take pains to instruct me, to restrain me, to warn me, to train me up or set me a good example. They corrupted my mind from my very infancy."

Many a wicked child will at that day be seen rising, accusing, and cursing his parents, and will continue to do so in torments to all eternity. Parents who have parental affections for their children, I would beseech you to seriously consider these things.

11

A Lovely and Pleasant Sight

(Given at the quarterly lecture, November 1744)

"That our sons may be as plants grown up in their youth, that our daughters may be as corner stones polished after the similitude of a palace." Psalm 144:12

David in this psalm prays that God would deliver him from his enemies, and speaks of the prosperity of God's people as the consequence of that deliverance, and pleads that he may be delivered so that God's people may prosper not only with temporal prosperity, but spiritual prosperity as well. This prosperity is summed up in the verse 15: "Happy is the people that is in such a case; yea, happy is that people whose God is the Lord."

So that David here seems here to speak of the happiness of Israel, or of the church, consisting in having the Lord for their God and depending on His deliverance. We are to understand David not speaking here so much in his own name as in the name of Christ.

The same is observable in other psalms where it is exceedingly evident that David speaks in the name of Christ, those psalms being applied to Christ in the New Testament. David in like manner speaks as the psalmist does of the prosperity of God's people as depending on His deliverance. So it is in Psalm 22:20–22: "Deliver my soul from the sword; my darling from the power of the dog. Save me from the lion's mouth, for Thou hast heard me from the horns of the unicorn. I will declare Thy name unto my brethren; in the midst of the con-

gregation will I praise Thee." And verse 26: "The meek
shall eat and be satisfied; they shall praise the LORD
that seek Him; your heart shall live forever."

And so in Psalm 69:32, 35–36: "The humble shall see
this and be glad; and your heart shall live that seek
God. For God will save Zion, and will build the cities of
Judah, that they may dwell there and have it in posses-
sion."

There is a twofold prosperity: spiritual and temporal. It is evident that the design of the psalmist is not
only to mention temporal prosperity by the conclusion.

The subject of the text is the spiritual prosperity of a
people as appearing very much in the piety of their
youth. The piety of the young is particularly mentioned
in the description of a people that are spiritual in flourishing circumstances, and that probably for these two
reasons:

1. The flourishing of religion among a people usually begins with the young people.

2. Because the virtue and piety of the youths are particularly in many respects peculiarly desirable, and is
much the beauty of a professing people of God.

The piety of the youth of a people is spoken of here
as beautiful and as a lovely sight to behold; and therefore those young people who are pious are here represented by those things that are beautiful to the beautiful and pleasant to the eye. Virtuous and pious young
men are compared to flourishing plants. Pious young
women are here compared to polished cornerstones.

Two things are here represented: First, their useful-
ness in the families they belong to, or their being
prospered and fitted to be eminently serviceable in
families as the cornerstone is of great use in the house.
This is agreeable to what the wise man says in Proverbs
14:1: "A wise woman buildeth the house." This is also
agreeable to the description he gives of the virtuous

woman in Proverbs 31.

Second, their being, by their piety, rendered peculiarly amiable, polished, after the similitude of a palace.

DOCTRINE: 'Tis a peculiarly lovely and pleasant sight to behold young people walking in the ways of virtue and piety.

It is a pleasant sight upon two accounts:

First, there is a peculiar decency in it. It is most suitable that men should begin their lives with God and dedicate the first of their time to Him. Youth is the flower of life and, on many accounts, the best part of it. And it is peculiarly becoming that this time should be devoted to God. When persons begin their lives with God, hereby the whole life is given to Him.

Second, it is a pleasing sight on account of the pleasing prospect it gives, of the benefit of it, and of the good fruits and consequences that it tends to bring. This is true inasmuch as it tends to prevent a great deal of sin; it gives a prospect of more eminent holiness. And persons, thereby being much more useful and beneficial in human society, are prepared to live in the world as members of society when they are fit before they enter on the stage, being more eminent in piety.

Application

USE OF EXHORTATION. When God demands of you that you give Him your youth, is it not a most reasonable demand? How ill your spending your youth in sin, and in a carnal, light, and vain manner agrees with your mortality. You may rationally conclude that some of you here will never have any other opportunity than the time of youth.

Many persons get that wound by the sins of youth that, if they live to grow old, they never get rid of, but it goes with them into the grave and into eternity. The guilt abides with them forever. God doesn't excuse them because they were in their youth. Ecclesiastes 11:9: "Rejoice, O young man, in thy youth; and let thy heart cheer thee in the days of thy youth, and walk in the ways of thine heart and in the sight of thine eyes; but know that for all these things God will bring thee into judgment."

God doesn't forget the sins of their youth, and they themselves are never ready in any great measure to forget them. Many others may forget them, but the guilt remains. They contract that badness of heart which is never removed, and oftentimes quench those motions of the Spirit that they have then and will never have them again. In youth those motions are more easily awakened. It is more common to have motions and stirrings of the Spirit while young than afterwards. But if they stifle them, they are missing the best time for the good of their souls. And since they never receive any saving good, their sins sit down with them.

In youth they contract those ill habits that stay with them, and Satan gets a footing and gains strength in their hearts. And God, in many respects, frowns upon them, and follows them and blasts them. And at last their sins of youth lie down with them in the dust.

Consider the peculiar advantages young people are under to obtain spiritual and eternally good blessings. The great Orderer and Disposer of all things seems to have laid out this season, as it were, for Himself. Youth is the freest opportunity and season as to time; later other business and concerns tend to crowd out religion. So this is the freest time, as to internal prejudices and obstacles, a time when persons more easily receive impressions from awakening sermons and awakening providences.

Afterwards it is abundantly easier to prejudice and

harden them if they have neglected religion because they are so much more used to those things that more often quench motions of the Spirit; if they continue longer in sin, then there are more frequent struggles with conscience because they are used to carnal reasonings and are guilty of often backsliding. God more easily grants His assistance and blessing to early endeavors. Proverbs 8:17: "Those that seek Me early shall find Me."

Consider, what advantage will it be to you to spend your youth in a carnal and vain manner? It may be that you promise yourself ease and pleasure. But you have mistaken notions of things; how poor, empty, and miserable is that pleasure these things are! 'Tis unreasonable and unbecoming a rational creature; it is base and bruitish. A man must put out the lights of his reason in order to enjoy them. They debase the nature, and then how empty they are, and in the end they give them no satisfaction. And then how vanishing are they; they are momentary and like a flash, a crackling of thorns (Ecclesiastes 7:6).

Youthful sins are pernicious. They tend in the end to destroy your outward comfort; if we take a view of the world and look upon those who have been most noted for spending their youth, they commonly are the most miserable of men.

Such a way of spending youth commonly lays a foundation for unquietness and discontentment; it tends to destroy the relish of outward enjoyments and in many ways mingles a bitterness with them.

I dare appeal to those young people who have in a great measure neglected religion, given the reins to their inclinations, and who have spent a great deal of their time in vain mirth and those diversions that are inconsistent with a serious religious, devout, and strict life. Judge and consider whether you have gotten any-

thing by it, all things considered; have you enjoyed
yourselves any better than if you had avoided all and
maintained a strict conversation on Sabbath days and
every other day?

The pleasures of religion are such as will not die
with youth; with respect to this life and its exercises and
enjoyment, they shall not decay. Rather, their bloom
and vigor will increase until they are perfected in glory.

Now, therefore, let me exhort and beseech you who
are the young people in the congregation to walk in
the ways of virtue and piety. Let this pleasant and beautiful sight be beheld in this town. It is pleasant not only
in the eyes of men, but in the sight of angels and of
God Himself.

This will be for the honor of the town of Northampton, and it will be greatly for your honor, and in
every way for your good and prosperity. A life of virtue
and piety is the way to be honorable; it is the way to be
useful and a blessing to mankind; it is the way to be
comfortable to parents and to all around you; it is the
way for you to be a blessing in the world, and it is the
way to be happy. In these things I dare to appeal to your
own reason, as I am speaking to reasonable creatures.

Therefore let me beseech you, for the sake of the interest and honor of religion, for the sake of the honor
and prosperity of the town, for the sake of the comfort
of your parents and friends, for God and Christ's sake,
and for your own sake, to come to a full determination
to depart from all the ways of youthful vanity, all licentious practices and sinful indulgence of carnal appetites, all vanity and licentiousness in company, all
lewd ways of using your tongue, all indulgence of a vain
and unclean imagination, all such liberties in company, and all such diversions, merriment, and night-
walkings as are not consistent with a close walk with
God, a heart devoted to God, and a life given to Christ.

That life should be spent in a serious, strict, daily pursuit of the great business of religion and a heavenly conversation.

Particularly be exhorted to spend this winter as becomes Christians and visible children of God. Spend your time for the good of your souls; let these long winter evenings be spent profitably. Don't cast off the counsels now given, and, notwithstanding all that can be said, don't waste this winter in a vain manner to the dishonor of God and the wounding of your soul.

Remember the solemn vows that many of you are under. You can't live a vain life at so cheap a rate as most others.

Let me beseech you prudently to seek your own happiness. 'Tis for your sake and not my own that I thus beseech you. It has long appeared to me a most amiable and desirable sight to see young people happy. I have therefore been exceedingly desirous that the young people of this town be religious early ever since I have been in the town. And as I desire your good and your happiness in this world and that which is to come, and as God has committed the care of your souls to me, I beseech you to hearken to me. If you do so you, will rejoice in it; you'll find the good of it in this world and will rejoice in another world; you will praise God to all eternity that ever such counsels were given you and that God gave you a heart to hearken to them.

Consider how happy those young persons must be who give up their youth to God and spend it in a strict walk in the ways of virtue and piety. This one thing may be enough to show that they are unspeakably happy in that they live in preparation for death. And while they live, they live vastly more pleasantly. They have more comfort; their youth is more pleasant and they have better pleasures.

They have a more excellent nature that is heavenly,

divine, solid, substantial, and more exquisitely delighting. They have the most excellent ornaments and pleasures of divine love and friendship. They have the
sweeter pleasure of society with Christ and with one
another. They have the sweetest gratification of appetites and their outward enjoyments are vastly sweeter
and better. Their life is pleasant in all its circumstances
and concerns, and they have the most pleasure whether
alone or in company.

12

The Awful Death of Unclean Youth

(Given at the quarterly lecture, November 1748)

"They die in youth, and their life is among
the unclean." Job 36:14

In this passage, observe the fearful end that they
come to at last, and note the two circumstances mentioned that render it so:
1. They die in youth.
2 . Their life is among the unclean.

**DOCTRINE: 'Tis a very awful thing for persons to
die in youth whose life has been among the unclean.**

In this brief talk I will, first, show when it may be
said that a person's life is among the unclean, and
then, second, give some reasons why it is an awful
thing for those to die in youth who have lived thus.

1. A person's life may be said to be unclean when
they live in any way of uncleanness; when they have unclean actions that tend to kindle, promote, or gratify
any lust of uncleanness. Ephesians 5:3: "But fornication, and all uncleanness, let it not be once named
among you . . . ." Galatians 5:19: "Now the works of the
flesh are manifest, which are these: adultery, fornication, uncleanness, lasciviousness . . . ." And according
to Ephesians 5:11–12, not only are we to have no fellowship with the unfruitful works of darkness, but rather
we are to reprove them. In fact, the apostle tells us that
it is "a shame even to speak of those things which are
done of them in secret." Romans 13:12–13: "Let us

141

therefore cast off the works of darkness, and let us put
on the armor of light. Let us walk honestly, as in the
day; not in rioting and drunkenness, not in
chambering and wantonness . . . ." Romans 1:24 says
that God gives men up to uncleanness, and verses 26–27
speak of God giving men up to vile affections, even to
things that are unnatural.

Unclean talk makes a person unclean. Ephesians
5:4: "Neither filthiness nor foolish talking, nor jesting." And Ephesians 4:29: "Let no corrupt communication proceed out of your mouth . . . ."

Unclean imaginations make a person unclean.
Matthew 15:19–20: "For out of the heart proceed evil
thoughts, murders, adulteries, fornications . . . these
defile a man." Proverbs 24:9: "The thought of foolishness is sin." Proverbs 15:26: "The thoughts of the
wicked are an abomination to the Lord, but the words
of the pure are pleasant words." Proverbs 23:7: "As he
thinketh in his heart, so is he."

Persons are unclean when they live in a way of keeping company with unclean persons. Proverbs 13:20: "A
companion of fools shall be destroyed." Ephesians 5:11
tells us to have no fellowship with the unfruitful works
of darkness. 1 Corinthians 5:9: "I wrote to you in a epistle not to keep company with fornicators."

2. Here I shall give reasons why it is an awful thing
for a young person to die in uncleanness.

First, uncleanness is a sin of dreadful tendency. It
brings great guilt; it is a very provoking sin to God.
Remember the sins of uncleanness in the old world.
Remember what happened to Sodom, to Onan, to
Hophni and Phinehas.

Uncleanness was one of the sins that brought God's
wrath on Jerusalem. Jeremiah 29:23: "Because they have
committed villany in Israel, and have committed adultery with their neighbors' wives . . . ."

Welcome to the Miller Branch

Customer ID: **********4709

Title: Three black swans
ID: 31267501141954
Due: 07/28/2014 23:59:59

Title: Code Orange
ID: 31267139412967
Due: 07/28/2014 23:59:59

Title: Double Digit
ID: 31267503765321
Due: 07/28/2014 23:59:59

Title: Marie Antoinette, serial killer
ID: 31267400074579
Due: 07/28/2014 23:59:59

Title: The beginning of everything
ID: 31267504086529
Due: 07/28/2014 23:59:59

Total items: 5
7/7/2014 11:31 AM

Howard County Library System
2013 Library of the Year
(Gale/Library Journal)

Jeremiah 5:7-9: ". . . they committed adultery, and assembled themselves by troops in the harlots' houses. They were as fed horses in the morning: every one neighed after his neighbor's wife. Shall I not visit for these things? saith the Lord; and shall not My soul be avenged on such a nation as this?"

Ezekiel 22:9-11: ". . . in the midst of thee they commit lewdness. In thee have they discovered their fathers' nakedness . . . and one hath committed abomination with his neighbor's wife; and another hath lewdly defiled his daughter in law; and another in thee hath humbled his sister, his father's daughter."

Such are spoken of by the apostles with a great many testimonies of abhorrence. Romans 1 shows that the heathen brought the wrath of God upon themselves for their fornication. Ephesians 5:3-6 shows that because of these things—fornication, uncleanness, covetousness, filthiness, foolish talking, jesting, and whoremongering—the wrath of God comes upon men. Such things defile the world.

The apostates who lived in the apostles' time had unclean eyes. 2 Timothy 3:6 says that such false teachers creep into houses and lead silly women captive, who are "laden with lusts." The Apostle Peter speaks of false teachers who "allure through the lusts of the flesh, through much wantonness." And the Apostle Jude describes them as turning the grace of our God into lasciviousness. He likens them to Sodom and Gomorrha in their "giving themselves over to fornication and going after strange flesh." He shows their uncleanness to be one of the provoking sins of antichrist.

Second, uncleanness has a peculiar tendency to harden the heart and to lead it into stupidity. Hosea 4:11: "Whoredom and wine and new wine take away the heart." Uncleanness makes men brutish. Men are even compared to brutes in Scripture. Jeremiah 5:8 compares men to fed horses. Revelation 22:15 compares them to dogs. 2 Peter 2:10 compares those "that walk after the flesh in the lust of uncleanness" to "natural brute beasts" in verse 12. And verse 14 says that because they have eyes full of adultery, they are cursed.

Third, uncleanness is spoken of as being a sin that in a peculiar manner excludes persons from heaven and exposes them to the flames of hell. Ephesians 5:5–6: "For this ye know, that no whoremonger nor unclean person . . . hath any inheritance in the kingdom of God. Let no man deceive you with vain words, because of these things cometh the wrath of God upon the children of disobedience."

1 Corinthians 3:17 warns men not to defile the temple of God. And it is for that reason they are commanded to flee fornication in 1 Corinthians 6:18–19. Plus we are told in Revelation 21:27 that nothing that defiles or works abomination shall enter heaven. And 22:15 says that "without are whoremongers."

2 Peter 2:9–10 contrasts the godly with "them that walk after the flesh in the lust of uncleanness." Proverbs 7:21–27 says that the way of uncleanness is the way to hell. And 9:13–17 shows that the unclean "are in the depths of hell."

Fourth, uncleanness peculiarly unfits the mind for things of a spiritual and holy nature. Proverbs 5:14, speaking of avoiding the strange woman, says that "I was almost in all evil."

Fifth, uncleanness will appear to be an awful thing when we consider what a speedy end is put to all their unclean pleasures, or if we consider those things that they are soon brought to, and how diverse they are from what were found in them before in their unclean life. See also how death disappoints all the desires and hopes of such unclean young people as have a long, continued enjoyment of carnal delights. Death also cuts persons off from that future opportunity of repentance upon which they so often presume. Death frustrates all opportunity for young people to fulfill their intentions.

Sixth, how rare a thing it is that such as have lived such a life have true repentance given to them at death.

Seventh, what a vast and sudden change is made by the damnation of such young people when they die impenitent.

Application

1. Let this doctrine put the young people upon self-reflection. Let it endeavor to dissuade young people from ruin.

2. Let this doctrine be a warning to the young people to take heed that their life isn't spent among the unclean youth. Youth is a time of great temptation. Multitudes of young people live such a life as we have spoken of. The consideration of your mortality, one would think, should be argument enough. God shows you in many instances how liable you are to die in youth. Death doesn't pick and choose those who are ready. There are doubtless thousands and millions now in hell who were not ready to die when death came.

Consider how your present unclean ways would probably appear to you on a deathbed if you should be seized in youth. And consider how these impure delights will steal away the best opportunity you will ever have for the good of your soul.

And even if you should not die in youth, and yet spend your life among the unclean in your youth, how little probability is there that you will ever truly repent? You will be like those spoken of in Jude 12, spots who are twice dead. Ecclesiastes 7:26 says that uncleanness is more bitter than death.

Consider how short-lived these impure delights are in length compared to the future torments that are commonly the consequence.

Consider also the solemn vows that are upon many of you.

Consider that this sin tends to bring God's curse upon you in this life. Such it did upon the house of Eli. There are far better pleasures to be enjoyed. There are lawful ways of using the enjoyments of this life that are far better than unlawful pleasures.

Consider the great rewards that are to be obtained in a way of denial of sensual appetites.

There are means to help you in this endeavor:

• Avoid evil companions.

• Don't spend a great deal of time in unprofitable company and diversions. Rather, keep virtuous and religious company. And keep up secret prayer.

• Avoid the appearances and approaches of evil; avoid those things that tend to sin. Proverbs 6:28: "Can one go upon hot coals and his feet not be burned?" And Jesus Christ Himself told us that "if thy right hand offend thee, cut it off."

Job 31:1: "I made a covenant with mine eyes; why then should I think upon a maid?"

13

The Danger of Sinful Mirth

(Given at a lecture-day evening meeting
in November 1734)

"For as the crackling of thorns under a pot, so is the
laughter of the fool. This also is vanity." Ecclesiastes 7:6

The wise man, from the second verse of this chapter
to this sixth verse, which is our text, insists on the vanity of carnal and sinful mirth. In verse 2 he says that it is
better to go to the house of mourning than to the
house of feasting; that is, it is better to go to a place of
sorrow and mourning than to a feast or banquet that is
intended only for merriment.

To the same purpose is verse 3: "Sorrow is better
than laughter." So vain is carnal mirth that even sorrow
itself, the most irksome thing to man's nature, is here
accounted preferable, and that because sorrow has a
tendency to make the heart better, but carnal mirth
only serves to make it worse. Verse 4: "The heart of the
wise is in the house of mourning, but the heart of fools
is in the house of mirth." A wise man who considers
things as they are would rather be in the house of
mourning than in the company of those who intend
only carnal mirth and jollity. His mind is more taken
up about those things that we are put in mind of in a
house of mourning; but the heart of fools is in the
house of mirth. It is a sign of an inconsiderate, foolish,
empty mind to be much taken up with vain mirth, and
to delight much in jovial company and the like.

And verse 5: "It is better to hear the rebuke of the wise than for a man to hear the song of fools." We would be better off to go and keep company with serious, pious persons, though they should give us serious warnings and reproofs, than to go into vain company to hear their jovial, lewd songs. And then come the words of our text: "For as the crackling of thorns under a pot, so is the laughter of the fool." By "the laughter of the fool" is meant carnal and sinful mirth and jollity; fools refer to wicked men.

The nature of carnal and sinful mirth is declared by a comparison; it is compared to the crackling of thorns under a pot, that is, to the sudden blaze and noise of thorns or some other such thing in the fire. By this comparison several things are signified:

1. The great appearance there seems to be of good in it. When thorns, or something else of that nature, are cast into a fire they make a great blaze and noise. So if we were to judge by the outward appearance and a slight view of carnal mirth, there is a great deal of pleasure and happiness in it. Spiritual pleasure doesn't make such a noise; it is more inward and secret. Proverbs 14:10: "A stranger doth not intermeddle with his joy."

2. Then there is emptiness, the vanishing, fading nature of it. As the fire of thorns, while it lasts, makes a great blaze and crackling, yet it soon goes out and disappears. There is but very little substance in the fuel to maintain the fire, and so it quickly goes out and ceases.

3. It signifies the hurtful nature of it. As the blaze of thorns lasts but a little while, and when it has gone out there is nothing left but ashes, the fuel being consumed, so it is with carnal mirth: though it gives an appearance of pleasure and happiness while it lasts, yet it always leaves the person in whom it is worse than it found him.

DOCTRINE: The pleasure of sinful mirth is a worthless, pernicious, vanishing, and hurtful pleasure.

I would briefly declare what I mean by sinful mirth. In the negative sense, I do not mean that all manner of diversion is sinful. There may be diversion that is innocent, and that in no way infringes on the rules of Christianity. Persons may divert themselves at proper seasons, in a proper measure, and in such a manner that shall in no way be unbecoming the gospel. There is such a thing as maintaining innocence and virtue in diversion. Diversion suitably used may be profitable to better fit and prepare us for the business and duty of serving God.

I don't mean to speak against all society of young people one with another, or indeed even all diverting society. There is a way in which persons may entertain each other and yet profit each other at the same time.

But by carnal and sinful mirth I mean all that mirth that is lewd and savors of any thing unclean. I am speaking of that mirth that takes place when persons make themselves merry with lascivious language or with unclean jesting. Ephesians 5:4: "Neither filthiness, nor foolish talking, nor jesting, which are not convenient." And Ephesians 4:29: "Let no corrupt communication proceed out of your mouth."

Sinful mirth takes place in unclean, lewd songs, when persons are often defiling their mouths with something filthy and unseemly. Much more does it take place when that mirth consists in unclean actions.

Profane mirth is that mirth that takes place when persons will be unsuitably light upon the Sabbath, when they make themselves merry with things of a sacred nature. They lightly jest about holy things, about the Scriptures, about God's ordinances, about religious duty, about conversion or conviction, any work of the Spirit on the heart, or any spiritual experiences or holy actions. This is horridly profane, when persons will make merry with such things. But such sort of mirth is all too common.

Sinful mirth is when persons sport themselves with the infirmities of others: when their mirth consists in deriding their neighbors, talking against others, mocking and ridiculing their natural infirmities, their moral faults, or the infirmities of age; when they delight to rake up all they can against persons and aggravate it, set it forth, make more of it than it is, and then make sport with it.

Unseasonable mirth is when persons are ill-timed. Sometimes persons especially need to mourn and go heavily, such as in times of public calamity. Lately there have been some awful providences in the place where we live. It has very lately been a time of the frowns of Providence on ourselves. And Ecclessiastes 3:4 says that there is a time to weep and a time to laugh.

There is such a thing as exceeding bounds in the degree of mirth. It is very unsuitable for poor, sinful, guilty, mortal creatures to show a want of solidity of mind and a sober sense of things; it shows a want of a due consideration of our sinfulness. It shows the vanity of the world and a lack of the sense of the great things of another world. Mirth may be to that degree very unbecoming of Christians.

Mirth becomes sinful when too much time is spent in it. Mirth and diversion are only designed to fit us for the duties of our general and particular callings, and therefore should not crowd them out or interfere with them. When much time is spent in it, it becomes vain, carnal mirth; it shows that we set our hearts too much upon it, especially when it crowds out duties of religion such as meditation, reading, secret prayers, when it hinders us from attending family prayer, or when it takes the mind off from these duties. When mirth has the superiority over religion, then it becomes carnal mirth.

I proceed now to show how this sort of pleasure is a worthless, vanishing, and pernicious pleasure.

This kind of mirth is worthless, offensive, base, brutish, and unworthy of reasonable creatures. It cannot afford any satisfaction; it doesn't answer the cravings of the soul; it doesn't suit men's spiritual, rational nature. Man was made for higher and more excellent delights. This kind of mirth won't give contentment; rather it makes for more. It puts the soul into a tumultous, uneasy frame.

It is not only a very poor, worthless delight while it lasts, but it soon vanishes away and leaves the soul utterly empty and destitute. Such sinful delights and pleasures are but momentary delights; they are like a flash that is suddenly out. They are vanishing and very short-lived in themselves; their own nature won't suffer them to be of any long continuance.

They are vanishing because those earthly things that were the fuel that maintains them are of a fading nature. How often is all the pleasure of carnal mirth spoiled by sickness or some sore bodily distress that God sends on persons, or by some other judgment which God brings. If the world smiles for a little while and gives occasion for carnal mirth, yet the smiles of the world are vanishing and short-lived things; and by and by they will be followed with frowns and darkness that spoil all such mirth.

What a miserable creature is a poor, carnal wretch who places all his happiness in carnal mirth! When he is brought under some affliction, he is sensible of how destitute such comfort is at such a time.

This pleasure is a vanishing pleasure because the body is vanishing; the vigor and strength of the body gradually vanishes as age comes on, and so carnal mirth is spoiled. Very often all vanishes in death before old age comes; when life vanishes, all vanishes and is put out in obscure darkness.

The pleasure of carnal mirth is a pernicious pleasure. It is not only worthless and does no good, but it does a great deal of hurt; it is of a ruinous nature. Though the pleasure is vanishing, yet the pernicious effects of it are not, but are lasting and durable; yea, very often they are everlasting.

This pleasure is of a pernicious nature as it is greatly to the dishonor of God, and, not only so, but it is most hurtful and destructive to the subject of it. It is pernicious as it tends to destroy a person's outward comfort. There is nothing that tends to do so more than carnal pleasure. If we take a view of the world and look upon persons who have spent their youth in carnal and sinful mirth and pleasures, they seem to be the most miserable of men; they never seem to enjoy themselves as others do. Such a way of spending youth commonly lays a foundation for disquietness and discontent. It destroys the relish of the comforts of this life. Besides that, it tends to destroy that person's credit and to bring disgrace.

And then, which is worse, it is of a pernicious nature because it is ruinous to the soul. Such pleasures are of a very hardening and stupifying nature. They tend to set a person at a great distance from a due sense of the great things of another world. They tend to confirm a habit of sensuality and to greatly indispose a person to all spiritual duties. Carnal pleasures greatly hinder the efficacy of the Word of God; they make a person unfit for secret prayer, for meditation, or for any duty of the closet.

Carnal pleasures give the devil a great advantage. They expose a person to innumerable temptations; they tend to fill the mind with sinful thoughts and impure imaginations, and they oftentimes lead to great sins and even to sinful courses that prove the eternal ruin of the soul. They expose persons to the judgment and wrath of the great God. Ecclessiastes 11:9: "Remember that for all these things God will bring thee into judgment."

Application

USE OF WARNING. Let this doctrine warn you against carnal mirth. I hope that there are none here but who are already disposed to hearken to this warning. I may charitably judge so by your coming to this meeting, but yet you doubtless will hereafter have many temptations to it. And even if now you are well disposed as to this matter, the religious dispositions that appear in young people are oftentimes as a morning cloud and as the early dew that soon goes away (Hosea 6:4).

Everyone of you therefore needs to take heed to himself, and I hope you will do so from the consideration of the worthlessless and insignificance of such mirth, and its being unbecoming. I hope you will avoid it as being unworthy of rational creatures, but especially that you will avoid it because of its hurtful, ruinous nature and its tendency to destroy comfort in this world and the soul to all eternity. Consider two things:

1. Consider that if you should addict yourself to carnal mirth, how bitter will be your reflections on it hereafter; it will be bitter to think of it another day. For a short moment's pleasure you will have a long reckoning. Such kinds of pleasure don't lay any foundation for peace or comfort in any one, or for any quietness in the conscience; on the contrary, they lay a foundation for an abundance of trouble and for inward uneasiness and torment.

This kind of pleasure may cause you a great deal of bitterness through the greatest part of your life; it may cause bitterness in old age. If ever your conscience afterwards should be awakened, how will the thoughts of it trouble you. And what bitter reflections will it probably cause when you come to die. When you lie under strong pain and feel nature languishing, will these carnal delights be any comfort to you then? Will it be a pleasure to you to think of them then? On the contrary, how sinking and terrfying will it be to look back upon it! Proverbs 5:11–13: "And thou mourn at the last, when thy flesh and thy body are consumed, and say, 'How have I hated instruction, and my heart despised reproof; and have not obeyed the voice of my teachers, nor inclined mine ear to them that instructed me.' " How dreadful will it be to you in hell to think that you were so foolish as for the sake of some carnal pleasure!

2. Consider that young people oftentimes, by the sins of carnal mirth and the extravagances of youth, get such a wound to the soul as they never get over as long as they live, but 'tis a wound that proves to be their ruin, a wound that proves mortal to them, a wound that carries them to hell. Job 20:11: "His bones are full of the sins of his youth."

They so provoke God that thereby He leaves them and never gives the gracious influences of His Spirit to them. Their hearts are so hardened in sin by such wounds given to the conscience that they never get over them; the habits of sin are so confirmed that they never forsake them; the guilt and pollution of their youthful sins stick by them and ever hinder the effect of all means. The Word and God's ordinances never prove effectual to them as long as they live. Their wound remains unhealed till they grow old and it goes with them to their graves into eternity.

USE OF EXHORTATION. Let this exhort you who are

here to seek the pleasures of a life of love for Christ and communion with Him. I hope you who have come here this night have come for this end, and I hope you will continue to meet together for this end, that you will also seek pleasure in all other proper ways, that you will henceforth make religion your great business, and that you won't be unsteady and inconstant, trifling in the affair of religion.

Let me beseech you to cast off all carnal mirth and sinful pleasure, and seek the sweet and excellent delights and pleasures that are to be had in a life of love for the Lord Jesus Christ and in communion with Him.

Consider how much better these pleasures are:

1. This pleasure is not mean and worthless, but of an excellent, a heavenly, a noble, and an exalted nature.

2. 'Tis a more sweet and satisfying sort of pleasure. You may sit down under Christ's shadow with great delight (Song of Solomon 2:3). His love is better than earthly love. Christ will manifest His love to you, and you will have conversation with Him. Christ has better delights to give you than the world can. Nothing here can express the sweetness of His love. You will desire no better, no other happiness. Psalm 63:5: "My soul shall be satisfied as with marrow and fatness."

3. This pleasure does not fade. John 4:13–14: "Whosoever drinketh of this water shall thirst again; but whosoever drinketh of the water that I shall give Him shall never thirst, but the water that I shall give him shall be in him a well of water springing up into everlasting life." He will have within him a living spring, always running, a stream that is never dry. When other streams have dried up, this one will supply you in times of famine. When temporal afflictions come upon you, this will stand you in good stead. Jeremiah 17:7–8: "Blessed is he that trusteth in the Lord, and whose hope the Lord is. For he shall be as a tree planted by

the waters, and that spreadeth out her roots by the river, and shall not see when heat cometh, but her leaf shall be green; and shall not be careful in the year of drought, neither shall cease from yielding fruit."

This happiness won't fail you when outward things fail, when your body fails, or when life fails. Psalm 73:26: "Though my heart and my flesh fail, yet God is the strength of my heart and my portion forever." These pleasures are true pleasures indeed.

4. These pleasures won't disturb your inward peace, but will give and establish it. You will have no bitter reflections; you will have no bitterness on your death bed, no bitterness in another world.

5. And these pleasures will be in no way hurtful to your nature. Sinful pleasures destroy as the fire of thorns. But these heavenly pleasures build up; they are health to the soul. They make the heart better, not worse; they leave a sweet relish and a holy disposition; they don't tend to ruin the soul, but, on the contrary, to fit and prepare it for the enjoyment of God. They give light to the understanding and a holy disposition to the will; they sanctify the affections and lay a foundation for peace and quiet, for comfort in this world and glory in the world to come.

14

A Letter to a Young Convert

(Sometime in 1741, a young lady residing in Smithfield, Connecticut, who had lately made a profession of religion, requested Mr. Edwards to give her some advice as to the best manner of maintaining a religious life. In reply, he addressed to her the following letter, which will be found eminently useful to all persons just entering on the Christian course.)

My dear young friend,

As you desired me to send you in writing some directions as to how to conduct yourself in your Christian course, I would now answer your request. The sweet remembrance of the great things I have lately seen at Smithfield inclines me to do anything in my power to contribute to the spiritual joy and prosperity of God's people there.

1. I would advise you to keep up as great a striving and earnestness in religion as if you knew yourself to be in a natural state and were still seeking conversion. We advise persons under conviction to be earnest and violent for the kingdom of heaven; but when they have attained to conversion, they ought not to be any less watchful, laborious, and earnest in the whole work of religion, but the more so; for they are under infinitely greater obligations. For want of this, many persons, in a few months after their conversion, have begun to lose the sweet and lively sense of spiritual things, and to grow cold and dark, and have pierced themselves through with many sorrows, whereas, if they had done

157

as the apostle did (Philippians 3:12–14), their path would have been as the shining light, that shines more and more unto the perfect day.

2. Do not leave off seeking, striving, and praying for the very same things that we exhort unconverted persons to strive for, and a degree of which you have already had in conversion. Pray that your eyes may be opened, that you may receive sight, that you may know yourself and be brought to God's footstool, that you may see the glory of God and Christ and be raised from the dead, and have the love of Christ shed abroad in your heart. Those who have most of these things have need to still pray for them; for there is so much blindness and hardness, pride and death remaining that they still need to have that work of God wrought upon them, further to enlighten and enliven them, that shall bring them out of darkness into God's marvelous light, and be a kind of new conversion and resurrection from the dead. There are very few requests that are proper for an impenitent man that are not also, in some sense, proper for the godly.

3. When you hear a sermon, hear for yourself. Though what is spoken may be more especially directed to the unconverted, or to those who in other respects are in different circumstances from yourself, yet let the chief intent of your mind be to consider, "In what respect is this applicable to me? And what application ought I to make of this for my own soul's good?"

4. Though God has forgiven and forgotten your past sins, yet do not forget them yourself; often remember what a wretched bondslave you were in the land of Egypt. Often bring to mind your particular acts of sin before conversion, as the blessed Apostle Paul is often mentioning his old blaspheming, persecuting spirit and his injuriousness to the renewed, humbling his heart, and acknowledging that he was the least of the

apostles, not worthy to be called an apostle, and the chief of sinners. Be often confessing your old sins to God, and let that text be often in your mind which is found in Ezekiel 16:63: " 'That thou mayest remember and be confounded, and never open thy mouth any more, because of thy shame, when I am pacified toward thee for all that thou hast done,' saith the Lord God."

5. Remember that you have more cause, on some accounts a thousand times more, to lament and humble yourself for sins that have been committed since conversion than before, because of the infinitely greater obligations that are upon you to live to God, and to look upon the faithfulness of Christ in unchangeably continuing His loving-kindness, notwithstanding all your great unworthiness since your conversion.

6. Be always greatly abased for your remaining sin, and never think that you lie low enough for it; but yet be not discouraged or disheartened by it for, though we are exceedingly sinful, yet we have an Advocate with the Father, Jesus Christ the righteous, the preciousness of whose blood, the merit of whose righteousness, and the greatness of whose love and faithfulness infinitely overtop the highest mountains of our sins.

7. When you engage in the duty of prayer, come to the Lord's Supper, or attend any other duty of divine worship, come to Christ, as Mary Magdalene did (Luke 7:37–38); come and cast yourself at His feet and kiss them, and pour forth upon Him the sweet, perfumed ointment of divine love out of a pure and broken heart, as she poured the precious ointment out of her pure, broken alabaster box.

8. Remember that pride is the worst viper that is in the heart, the greatest disturber of the soul's peace and of sweet communion with Christ; it was the first sin committed, and lies lowest in the foundation of Satan's whole building; it is with the greatest difficulty rooted

out, and is the most hidden, secret, and deceitful of all lusts, often creeping insensibly into the midst of religion, sometimes under the guise of humility itself.

9. That you may pass a correct judgment concerning yourself, always look upon those as the best discoveries and the best comforts that have the most of these two effects: those that make you least and lowest, and most like a child, and those that most engage and fix your heart in a full and firm disposition to deny yourself for God, and to spend and be spent for Him.

10. If at any time you fall into doubts about the state of your soul, in dark and dull frames of mind, it is proper to review your past experience; but do not consume too much time and strength in this way. Rather apply yourself, with all your might, to an earnest pursuit after renewed experience, new light, and new lively acts of faith and love. One new discovery of the glory of Christ's face will do more to scatter clouds of darkness in one minute than examining old experience, by the best marks that can be given, for a whole year.

11. When the exercise of grace is low, and corruption prevails, and, by that means, fear prevails, do not desire to have fear cast out by any other way than by the reviving and prevailing of love in the heart. By this, fear will be effectually compelled, as darkness in a room vanishes away when the pleasant beams of the sun are let into it.

12. When you counsel and warn others, do it earnestly, affectionately, and thoroughly; and when you are speaking to equals, let your warnings be intermixed with expressions of your own unworthiness, and of the sovereign grace that makes you differ.

13. If you would set up religious meetings of young women by themselves, to be attended once in a while besides the other meetings that you attend, I should think it would be very proper and profitable.

14. Under special difficulties, or when in great need of, or great longings after, any particular mercy for yourself or others, set apart a day for secret prayer and fasting; and let the day be spent not only in petitions for the mercies you desire, but in searching your heart, and in looking over your past life and confessing your sins before God—not as is wont to be done in public prayer, but by a very particular rehearsal before God of the sins of your past life, from your childhood hitherto, before and after conversion, with the circumstances and aggravations attending them, spreading all the abominations of your heart very particularly, and as fully as possible, before Him.

15. Do not let the adversaries of the cross have occasion to reproach religion on your account. How holy should the children of God, the redeemed and the beloved of the Son of God, behave themselves. Therefore, "walk as children of light and of the day," and "adorn the doctrines of God your Savior." Especially, abound in what are called the Christian virtues, and which make you like the Lamb of God; be meek and lowly of heart, and full of pure, heavenly, and humble love to all; abound in deeds of love to others, and self-denial for others; and let there be in you a disposition to account others better than yourself.

16. In your course, walk with God and follow Christ as a little, poor, helpless child, taking hold of Christ's hand, keeping your eye on the marks of the wounds in His hands and side whence came the blood that cleanses you from sin, and hiding your nakedness under the skirt of the white, shining robes of His righteousness.

17. Pray much for the ministers and the church of God, especially, that He would carry on the glorious work which He has now begun till the world shall be full of His glory.

15

Bible Questions for the Children of Northampton

(The questions here presented are just as they were in the original manuscript, except for the child's name.)

1. Which of the kings of Israel and Judah was it that reigned longest? (Manasseh)

2. What was his name who was David's ancestor that we read of as being in the wilderness with Moses?

3. How often was the family of the kings of Israel changed, or how often did the crown of the ten tribes go from one family to another before the captivity of the ten tribes?

4. God threatened Eli in 1 Samuel 2, especially in verses 30 and 35, that the priesthood should depart from his house or posterity to another family. When was that fulfilled?

5. It was threatened in Joshua 6:26 that he who should build Jericho again should lay the foundation in his first born. Where was that fulfilled? (Hiel the Bethelite, 1 Kings 16:34).

6. Whose posterity were the Midianites, and what relation was Midian, the father of the Midianites, to Abraham?

7. What relation was Amalek, the father of the Amalekites, to Jacob?

8. Whose posterity were the Ammonites?

9. Whose son was Moab, the father of the Moabites?

10. Whose posterity were the Assyrians?

11. Job is said to live in the land of Ur. Whose son was Ur, in whose land Job lived?

12. How many altars were in use in the tabernacle?

13. They were wont in Israel to keep the day of the new moon as a solemn day. Where in the law of Moses is this commanded? (Numbers 10:10 and 28:11)

14. Who was the father of the Hittites, from when they had their name? (see Genesis 23)

15. Whose posterity were those Kenites that we read of in 1 Samuel 15:6?

16. In what tribe was Samaria?

17. Which of the three sons of Noah did the Egyptians come from?

18. How many years before Jacob was born did Shem die?

19. Who was the last man of Noah's line that was born so early that he might have seen Shem?

20. How many years before the flood was it that Enoch was translated?

21. How long or who of Noah's ancestors lived nearest to the time of the flood, or who of them died last?

22. How many cities of refuge were there in Israel? (6, Joshua 20)

23. What prophets do we read of that prophesied after the children of Israel were carried captive into Babylon?

24. What prophets do we read of that prophesied after the return of the children of Israel from their captivity into Babylon?

25. How many kings reigned in Judah after the captivity of the ten tribes? (8)

26. In what tribe was the city of Hebron? (Joshua 15:14; Joshua 14:14; 1 Chronicles 6:55; Joshua 21:11)

27. How many of the kings of Israel and Judah do we read of who died violent deaths? (Saul, Nadab—1 Kings 15:27; Elah—16:8; Zimri—v.18; Ahab, 1 Kings 22; Jehoram and Ahaziah, 2 Kings 9...in all, 16).

28. What king was it who first built the city of Samaria? (see 1 Kings 16:24)

29. Why was the city where the kings of Israel were wont to reside called Samaria, or whence was that name derived? (see 1 Kings 16:24)

30. Who was the owner of the ground on which the city of Samaria was built before the building of the city?

31. Which of the kings of Israel was it that first built the temple of Baal in Samaria that introduced the worship of Baal into Israel? (Ahab, 1 Kings 16:30-31)

32. How many sorts of creatures do we read of were there who were appointed to be offered in sacrifice by the Levitical law? (Neat cattle, sheep, goats, doves, sparrows, young pigeons.)

33. How many times do we read of sacrifice being offered or altars being built upon any occasions before Moses' time? (Abel, Noah, Genesis 8:20; Abraham, Genesis 12:7–8)

34. How many prophets do we read of who prophesied in the time of the judges?

35. When was the time when the generality of the children who were born in the nation of Israel for many years were left uncircumcised, and where do we have an account of it? (Joshua 5, at the beginning)

36. How many places were there in the land of Israel at which it was ordinary lawful to offer sacrifices?

37. How many altars had the whole nation of the Jews that they, by divine appointment, were to offer their burnt offerings upon?

38. Was the ark that was in Solomon's temple the same that was made by Moses' direction in the wilderness? (see 1 Kings 8:9)

39. How long, or until what time, was the brazen serpent that Moses made in the wilderness kept among the children till Hezekiah's time?

40. How many do we read of Christ raising from the dead? (3)

41. How many persons do we read of in the Old Testament who were raised from the dead? (3, 1 Kings 17:21; 2 Kings 4:24; 2 Kings 13:21)

42. Which is the biggest army of men that we read of in Scripture history of whose numbers we have some particular account, unless it be Jehosophat's army? (see 2 Chronicles 17:14ff)

43. Which is the biggest slaughter in one battle that we read of in Scripture history? (see 2 Chronicles 3:17)

44. Which is the biggest destruction of men made at once by the immediate, miraculous hand of God that we read of in Scripture history?

45. What king reigned the longest of any of the kings of Israel or Judah?

46. How many of the kings of Israel and Judah have we an account of come to their ends by violent means or were killed by the hands of men?

47. Which is the greatest slaughter of men in battle that we have an account of in Scripture? (Jereboam's army)

48. Which is the greatest slaughter of men made at one time by a supernatural hand of heaven that we have an account of in Scripture history? (Sennacharib's army, flood)

49. How many women was there then in Israel who were advanced to the chief seat of government? (Deborah and Atheliah)

50. Who was the youngest kind who we have an account of that ever reigned in the land of Canaan? (Joash, the son of Ahaziah; see 2 Chronicles 24:1)

51. It was prophesied that Esau, when he was strong, should shake off Jacob's yoke from off his neck. When was that fulfilled?

52. How often have we an account of the temples being pillaged of its treasure from the time that it was built till it was burnt by the Chaldeans? (8 times: 1 Kings 14:26; 1 Kings 15:18; 2 Kings 12:18; 2 Kings 14:14; 2 Kings 16:8; 2 Kings 18:15; 2 Kings 24:13; and when it was burnt by Nebuzardan)

53. Who was the youngest king of whose age we have any account in Scripture? (Joash, the son of Ahaziah in 2 Chronicles 24:1)

54. Whose posterity were the Sidonians, after whose name the city of Sidon was called?

55. How many sorts of things in Israel were there that might not be sold or alienated so but that they must return in the year of Jubilee?

56. How often was it appointed that the law should be read in the audience of the whole congregation of Israel? (Once in 7 years, Deuteronomy 30 or 31)

57. How many have we an account of in Scripture who fasted forty days and forty nights? (Moses, Joshua, Elijah, 1 Kings 19:8 and 10)

58. We read of 7 nations that inhabited the land of Canaan before the children of Israel, viz. the Amorites. Which of these seven nations inhabited the city of Jerusalem before it was possessed by...? (1 Chronicles 11:4; Judges 1:21)

59. What other name had the city that was called the city of palm trees? (Deuteronomy 34:3; 2 Chronicles 28:15)

60. Where was the place where the tabernacle was first fixed after the children of Israel settled in the land of Canaan? (Joshua 18:1)

61. Of what tribe were the inhabitants of the cities of refuge belonging? (Numbers 35:6 and Joshua 21)

62. In what tribes in Israel had the priests cities alloted to them? (Judah, Simon, and Benjamin–Joshua 21:4; also 13–19)

63. What is the most noted city for giants that we read of in Scripture?

64. How many of the kings of Israel or Judah do we read of who were anointed? (Saul, David, Solomon, Jehu, Jehoash   2 Kings 11:12)

65. How often was David anointed king? (3 times by Samuel, once at Hebron by Judah, 2 Samuel 2:4 by all Israel; 1 Chronicles 11:3)

66. How many sorts of officers do we read of in Scripture that were anointed to their office by God's appointment?

66. We read in Leviticus 23 that the Jews were required on the Feast of Tabernacle on the 15th day of the seventh month to dwell in booths made of the boughs of green trees. For how long a time was that custom neglected in Israel? (see Nehemiah 8:16–17)

67. Have we an account of the age of any man from Adam to Jacob, but what was one from whom Jacob descended or one of Jacob's forefathers? (Yes, Ishmael, in Genesis 25:17)

68. Who owned the land where the temple was built before it was set apart for that use? (see 2 Chronicles 3:1)

69. In what king's reign was the worship of Baal first established in the kingdom of Judah? (Jehorah, see 2 Chronicles 21. He married Athaliel, the daughter of Ahab.)

70. How often did the children of Israel come to the Red Sea after they departed from Mt. Sinai before they came to Canaan? (see Numbers 6:33; 14:25; Deuteronomy 2:1; 1 Kings 9:26)

71. Which of the epistles of the Apostle Paul is it that seems by what is contained in it to have been written a little before his death?

72. Who was the first that we have any account of in Scripture who was raised from the dead? (The widow's son of Zarephath, 1 Kings 17:21)

73. How many have we an account of that the Scripture mentions by name who have already risen from the dead to die no more?

74. How many have we a particular account of in Scripture who were raised from the dead?

75. How many have we an account of in Scripture that Christ raised from the dead while He was upon earth?

76. How many of the psalms were evidently penned before David had a being?

77. Who is the last prophet before Christ of whom we have account of whose ministry was accompanied and confirmed by miracles? (Daniel)

78. How many men have we an account of in Scripture who were immediately struck dead on the account of an irreverent use of the ark? (The men of Bethshemesh and Urzah, 1 Samuel 6:19. Total of 50, 071)

79. How many men do we read of that Christ raised from the dead before His crucifixion?

80. Who is he in the land of Canaan of whom we have account of the greatest numbers of kings subdued by him? (see Judges 1)

81. How many kings of Egypt have we an account of who was not called Pharaoh?

82. In what tribe was Libnah? (see 1 Chronicles 6:57)

83. In what tribe was Lachish?

84. How often have we an account of Christ's working the miracle of opening the eyes of the blind? (6: Matthew 9:27; Mark 8:22; Matthew 20:30; Mark 10:46; Luke 7:21; Matthew 12:22; John 9:1)

85. How often have we an account of Christ's stilling the winds and the sea? (2: Matthew 8:26; Mark 5:30; Luke 8:24; Matthew 14:32; Mark 6:51; John 6:21)

86. Is there any prophecy in Scripture that holds forth that Christ should be raised from the dead in a short time after he was put to death? (Psalm 16:10)

87. Where is the prophecy which above all others in the OT seems most to point forth the kind of death that Christ was to be put to? (Psalm 22:16)

88. In what places is it foretold that Christ would open the eyes of the blind? (Jonah, Isaiah 20:18; Isaiah 35:5; Isaiah 42:17–18)

89. How often do we have an account of Christ curing deaf persons? (2: Mark 7:32; Mark 9:25; Matthew 11:5; Luke 7:22)

90. Were there any persons besides the priests and Levites who were not of the seed of Israel and of the tribe of Levi who were allowed by their stated office or custom to do any service about the tabernacle and temple? (Gibeonites: Joshua 9:23, 27; Ezra 8:20)

91. How many of the sons of Jacob's posterity belong to the kingdom of Judah after Jereboam's revolt? (Levites: 2 Chronicles 11:13)

92. How many prophets have we an accout of whom we are either implicitly or expressly taught that they were masters or heads of the schools of the prophets?

93. Which is the greatest precise number that is anywhere mentioned in Scripture?

94. How often have we an account in Scripture of the OT prophets who dwelt in Canaan being sent out of their land to deliver messages to any other nations? (Jonah)

95. Who is the man who is mentioned in Scripture who is most generations distant from the Jews' return from the Babylonian captivity?

96. How many particular and distinct seas do we read of in the history of the OT?

97. What memorable transaction was there among the Israelites at that time of the year and month when the feast of weeks or Pentecost was kept in commemoration of which that festival seems therefore to be appointed?

98. Which way from Judea was the land of the Philistines? Was it towards the east, west, north, or south? (see Isaiah 11:14)

99. Which way from the land of Canaan lay the sea that in Scripture is called "the Great Sea"? (Joshua 15:2; Numbers 24:6)

100. Which was the most remarkable and plain testimony that Christ gave that He was the antitype of the sacrifices by any act or deed of His that we have an account of in the OT?

101. Who is the man who is mentioned in the OT who lived after the return from the captivity who lived most generations distant from it? (See 1 Chronicles 3, latter end, and Nehemiah 10:22)

102. Have we an account in the OT of any extraordinary warlike exploit of the tribe of Simeon after the time of the judges? (1 Chronicles 4, latter end)

103. Which was the last that we read of who was ever in any war against the Amalekites towards the fulfilling that threat in Exodus 17:14? (See 1 Chronicles 4, latter end)

104. Of how many tribes were there men appointed who were by their office to be singers and musicians in the house of God? (see Ezra 3:10; 1 Chronicles 16 and 6:31)

105. God threatened Eli in Samuel 2 at the latter end
that He would take away the high priesthood from his
family. When was that fulfilled? (1 Kings 2:27; 1 Kings
2:35

   Zadok was the son of Eleazar and Phinehas,
   1 Chronicles 6:50ff

   Eli was of Ithamar, 1 Chron 24:3, 6 compared with
   1 Samuel 14:3 and 22:9, 11, and 20)

106. Whose posterity of Aaron's sons was Zadok, who
Solomon made high priest? (see 1 Chronicles 6:50ff
and 1 Chronicles 6:4ff)

107. What prophecy was that terrible destruction of
priests that we read of in 1 Samuel 22? (On accomplish-
ment, see v. 11 of that chapter and compare it with 14:3)

108. Have we any acount in Scripture of any extraordinary warlike exploit of the tribe of Reuben at any
time after they were settled in their own land?
(1 Chronicles 5:10)

109. What was the first miracle that Christ wrought?

110. What was the greatest number who saw Christ after
he was risen?

111. Of what tribe was Hur, who was with Moses and Aaron in the wilderness? (see Exodus 31:2; 1 Chronicles 2:18–20)

112. Jacob, in his blessing of Joseph, says from thence is the shepherd the stone of Israel. What was there at any time in the tribe of Joseph that we may look upon as a fulfillment of that?

113. Jacob, in his blessing of Dan, says that Dan shall judge his people as one of the tribes of Israel. What does the Scripture history give us an account of that we may look upon as fulfillment of that prophecy?

114. Which is the last that we read of any of the children of Barzillai, the Gileadite who came with David? (Nehemiah 7:63)

115. How many men have we an account of in Scripture who were Nazarites?